LIFE THOUGHTS,

GATHERED FROM THE

EXTEMPORANEOUS DISCOURSES

OF

HENRY WARD BEECHER.

BY ONE OF HIS CONGREGATION.

THIRTIETH THOUSAND.

BOSTON:
PHILLIPS, SAMPSON AND COMPANY.
1859.

ELECTROTYPED AT THE
BOSTON STEREOTYPE FOUNDRY.

PREFACE.

SOME two years since, while visiting friends in a distant city, they proposed that I should take notes for them of Mr. Beecher's sermons. Upon my return I commenced doing so, without a thought of their going beyond the little circle for whom they were first intended. But, as page after page was added to my note-book, and read occasionally to one and another, it began to be suggested that they ought not to be confined to the few, but should be published in a volume and given to the many. Thus the present book came into being.

With rare exceptions, these notes have been taken from the Sabbath sermons and Wednesday evening lectures, since the date at which they were commenced. Most of them have never been written till now; for Mr. Beecher's best thoughts are not usually those which are beforehand committed coolly to paper; they are those which spring from the inspiration of the moment, and have no record save in the memory of his hearers. To gather up and preserve some of the treasures thus lavishly scattered, has been the aim of this volume. It is not given to the world as the full-boughed tree; but only as some of the leaves which have fallen from it through two successive seasons.

To Robert D. Benedict, Esq., of Brooklyn, whose own notes, taken during the same time, were placed at my disposal, I desire to express my cordial thanks.

EDNA DEAN PROCTOR.

BROOKLYN, N. Y., April, 1858.

INDEX.

Absent, speaking of the, 142.
Acorns, growth of, 32.
Actions, the best, often unconscious, 13.
Adversity, influence of, 24 ; — likened to winter winds, 84.
Æsthetical faith, 254.
Affection, 228 ; — parental, 195 ; — a tribute to God, 255.
Affliction, a guide, 49.
Afflictions, the uses of, 109.
African race, the, 166.
Agassiz, 248.
Aim, how to take, 188.
Alexandrian library, destruction of, 46.
" All right," 280.
Allston, his unfinished pictures, 123.
Almoners of God's bounty, 33.
Amazon, the stream of the, 138.
Ambition, 138 ; — when laudable, 112 ; — true, 256.
American people, the, nomadic, 272.
Amusements, under the devil's care, 185.
Anger, the, of truth and love, 156 ; — likened to tinder, 157 ; — truth spoken in, 190.
Anglo-Saxon, the skin of the, 165.
Animal nature, the, to be subjected, 75.
Apartments of the soul, 18.
Apothecary shop, an, 256.
Appetite, refinement of, 142.
Architect, God the, 227.
Armor-scourers, 200.
Arrow, thought is the, 67 ; — in God's bow, 139.
Arrows, trials compared to, 195.
Artillery practice, 173.
Artist, at work, 215 ; — copying a picture, 270.
Asceticism, 184, 236.
Aspiration, 138 ; — not incompatible with contentment, 117.
Association of ideas, power of, 69.
Associations, power of, 141.
Aster, late blossoming of the, 130.
Atlas, carrying the world, 43.
Attainments, not for ourselves, 41.
Attempts, accepted, 122.

Babe, the mother's anchor, 122.
Babes feed on the mother's bosom, 244.
Baggage, cares likened to, 146.
Bankruptcy, when it is blessed, 72.
Banner, unused, 235.
Bather, the sea receiving a, 103.
Battery, public sentiment a, 192.
Battle, life a, 200.
Beauty, the lavishness of, 243.
Bed, the, 143.
Beethoven, Psalm 73 likened to symphony of, 82.
Beggar, a flower from a, 154.
Belief, sincerity in, not enough, 16.
Bell, tolling of, for the lost, 127 ; — in a belfry, 257.
Benevolence, for sake of praise, 81 ; —

a *

abroad and at home, 204; — the highlands of, 235.
Bible, the, injured by commentators, 3; — a garden despoiled by beasts, 50; — a field of battle, 50; — the emotive truths of, 58; — man's duty not dependent on the, 149; — a ruin, 193; — the poetry and beauty of the, 221; — infidel views of the, 225; — its truths like gold in the soil, 242; — a trellis, 262.
Bible Society, the, 184.
Bird, mourning over the bursting shells of its eggs, 15.
Birds, thoughts likened to, 50; — frightened from a tree, 57; — building by rivers, 59; — fly above the dust, 91; — joys seek us like, 103; — men likened to, 161; — ready to migrate, 177; — feeding, 263; — the migration of, 278.
Blessing for cursing, 274.
Blindness, 278.
Blossoms, superfluous, 24; — not the emblems of religion, 37.
Boat, illustration from rowing a, 174.
Boring for a fountain, 298.
Boswell's Life of Johnson, 45.
Botany, the author's study of, 272.
Bow, feeling is the, 67; — anger, a, 190.
Boy, with ball of twine, 210.
Brahmins, the, 244.
Brake on a car wheel, 62.
Bread, Christ the, 125.
Bread of God, the, for which we pray, 52.
Bridge, experience a, 288.
Bridging a stream, 45.
Brokers, exchange, some preachers only, 65.
Buds, dread of unfolding, 147; — the expansion of, 196.
Building without plan, 161.
Buildings, the prosperity of men compared to the rearing of, 113.
Business, religion in, 209, 286.
Buoys in our course, 55.
Butterfly, a, 179.
"But then," 185.
Cable, a fifty foot, 237.
Caldron, the earth a, 150.
California, an emigrant to, 293.
Calvinism, its influences, 40.
Camelia, blooming of a, 295.
Canary bird, the singing of a, 282.
Candle burning, a nervous man compared to a, 191.
Cares, earthly, how the heart may fly above, 91.
Cathedral, a, more than cold stone, 12.
Cathedrals, forest, 102; — the spires unfinished, 162.
Cave of Kentucky, 280.
Cellar, a potato growing in a, 292.
Cerberus, in America, 184.
Chance, nothing happens by, 17.
Changes, never foretold or anticipated, 30.
Character, likened to porcelain, 175; — compared to a river, 291.
Charity, not in giving crumbs, 63; — to be bestowed in secret, 82; — grudging, 251.
Cheerfulness, 288.
Chestnuts, some Christians like, 212.
Child, plucking dewy grass and flowers, 35; — choking with passion, 38; — preparation for the care of a, 247; — in bed, on a stormy night, 297.
Children, dying young, like spring bulbs, 31; — as spools, 59; — reared under glass, 59; — ruined by parental indulgence, 72; — their birth, education, and influence on their parents, 119; — the loss of, 122; — grow to the likeness of parents, 136; — frightened in sleep, 170; — death of, 187; — our love to, 199; — the way to bring up, 218; — government of, 262.
Chimneys, smoky, 205.
China, war in, 245.
Cholera, not to be cured by studying theories, 2.
Chords, sweeter after discords, 61.
Christ, how to get a correct view of, 25; — regret for the loss of any of the words of, 46; — the foundation, 59; — the helmsman, 65; — on earth longed for, 76; — incarnation of, 77; — as-

cension of, 77; — the way, 93; — rising over the sea of our sinfulness, 118; — symbolized in the various parts of the house, 125; — all are kinsmen through, 133; — unpatriotic, 136; — prayer to, for the world, 151; — what gifts are acceptable to, 155; — not the pauper, 185; — the affection of, 195; — the Shepherd, 197; — a talisman, 207; — his love for us, 208; — his life not an official mission, 209; — and the Syro-Phœnician woman, 211; — his suffering vicarious, 221; — the absolute one, 248; — the fountain, 248; — prayers to, 249; — is God, 249; — the body of, 263.

Christian, the, his heart, like a lake, 73; — a two-foot, 90; — the voices of nature to the, 179; — all good belongs to the, 184; — a, in endeavor, 216; — where a man can be a, 220; — the joyful experience of the, 229; — a luminous, 288; — under bondage to fear, 296; — like a man in a castle on a stormy night, 297.

Christian character, likened to a wain laden with sheaves, 13; — compared to full fruit trees, 13.

Christian joy, like full harmony, 131.

Christian life, sometimes late in flowering, 130; — always the same, 142; — should be always tropical, 188; — a new river, 260; — evidences of a, 269.

Christian merchant, the, 219.

Christian truth, its power in unity, 53.

Christians, like railroad station houses, 22; — many-colored, 54; — likened to birds on the tree tops, 57; — known by the tokens of divine intercourse, 71; — their virtues, 123; — without distinction of sect, 150; — the obligations upon, 157; — like chestnuts, 212; — not all within the church, 2'5; — what the honest prayers of some would be, 251; — like the children of missionaries, 265; — like flowers at morning, 267; ignorant of their real nature, 273; — should acknowledge Christ, 275; — fearful, like blanched potato vines, 292; — as emigrants, 293; — likened to pilot boats, 293.

Christianity may exist in heresy, 25; helpful, 31; — its vertical power, 159; — to make men robust, 202; — its care for the weak, 241; — the might of the world on the side of, 244.

Church, reason for joining the, 19; — the proper atmosphere of, 22; — the, God's window, 32; — the, a court house, 46; — two classes of people in the, 47; — led by God from one *ism* to another, 57; — danger of absolute unity of belief in a, 167; — fear to disturb the peace of the, 173; — faithless, 188; — heresy in the, 249; — reasons for joining a, 259; — a nursery, 259; — a hospital, 259; — a lighthouse, 277; — duty of a man in a, 288.

Church and state in New England, 42.

Churches should not inspire awe, 20; — infidelity of, 42; — their enterprise in youth, 60; — like insurance companies, 200.

"Cineraria," 273.

Cisterns, artificial, 153.

Citizen, the, cannot renounce his duty to the public, 64; — the pabulum of the state, 173.

Citizens, children make men better, 119.

Clearing-up shower, the, 91.

Clock, the pendulum necessary to the movement of, 22; — in a belfry, sentimental religion likened to, 287.

Clocks, to be wound up, 129.

Coin of Christ's kingdom, the, 25.

Colleges, driven westward, 272.

"Come, ye blessed," 294.

Commentators, 3; — likened to insects, 210.

Communion, invitation to, 149; — a wedding, 202; — table, birds likened to Christian at the, 263.

Compensation, in the blending of joy and sorrow, 222.

Competence, a five-story, 2.

Conceited men, 245.

Confession of sins, 23; — of faults, 38; — disarms reproof, 44.
Congregational singing, 29, 129.
Congregationalism a propagator of liberty, 39; — in New England in early times, 42.
Connecticut valley, mists in the, 140.
Conscience, 294; — a sword, 29; — pettifogging in the court of, 36; — without perspective, 197; — interest of merchants in, 106; — the moaning of, 251.
Consecration to God, 223.
Conservative young men, 221.
Content, true meaning of, 113; — not incompatible with aspiration, 116; — rare, 165.
Conversion, illustrated by a clock, 22; — not necessarily terrible, 183; — a selfish, 267.
Conviction of sin, 151.
Convictions, speaking according to, 138.
Corner stone, Christ the, 125.
Cradle, the, 122.
Cream, to pray, 64.
Creation, from the fulness of God's thought, 102; — of worlds, 228.
Creditor, a snarling, 206.
Creed, likened to Jacob's ladder, 173.
Creeds, the war of, 217.
Cricket overturned by a plough, 159.
Crises, moral, 93; — commercial, 208.
Critics likened to scavengers, 53.
Croton water pressing on every faucet, 105.
Cryptogamous, our heart life, 120.
Cultivation, evils of excessive, 218.
Cunning overreaches itself, 52.
Curses, often only blessings grown mouldy, 25; — men love to nurse their, 145.
Cynics in morals, 53.

Death of children, 31; — of relations, consolation for the, 32; — a new life, 37; — how God bridges the stream of, 45; — likened to a bud bursting into flower, 59; — to the troubled Christian is the clearing-up shower, 91; — the beginning of our vacation, 96; — the dropping of the flower, 167; — welcome, 176; — a cheerful view of, 189; — like the fall of the leaf, 201; — joy in view of, 213; contemplation of, 235; — a rest, 257; — likened to launching a ship, 262; — likened to the migration of birds, 278.
December, the short day in, 261.
Defeat, a school, 35; — sometimes as sweet as victory, 108.
Destroyers, certain animals appointed as, 53.
Detraction, 143.
Development, to stop, 160.
Dew upon flowers, 177.
Difficulties, God's teachers, 227.
"Dim religious light," 47.
Discords belong only to this life, 19; — the use of, 61.
Dissimulation, 139.
Doctrinal preaching, 185.
Doctrine, the skin of truth, 97; — unwelcome, 193; — perversions of, 205.
Drawing lessons, 245.
Dulness, sobriety is not, 182.
Duty, universal, 157; — to the present, 181.
Duties of life likened to the swinging of a pendulum, 23.
Dwarf oak, a puny Christian likened to a, 89.

Eclipses, our hearts in, 123.
Egg, development from the, 255.
Election, the doctrine of, 174.
Elect, the, 241.
Emotion, influence of, on the intellect, 86.
Emphasis, 197.
Enemy, to love an, 274.
Engineer of a train, 276.
Engine, marine, reversal of, by a child, 16.
Enterprises, the growth of, likened to plants, 48.
Eternal, what things are, 85; — punishment, 196.
Etna, the sides of, 134.

Evaporation, the uses of, 226.
Events not discordant, 198.
Evidences, Christian, 269.
Excellence, relative, 161; — not negative, 182.
Exchange, the, 165.
Excitement, moral, 87; — the soul's hours of, 88.
Exclusiveness, 136, 199, 218.
Excuses, 151.
Exhausted receiver, an, 141.
Experience not uniform, 110.
Experiences, each man thinks his own peculiar, 5.
Exploring party, 87.
Eyes, sect of, 53.

Faces, dark, not an evidence of grace, 120.
Faculties, the, compared to windows in a village at night, 27; — are not furniture, 66; — balance of the, 179; — harmony of the, 279.
Failure of men in large business, 92.
Fairy structures, 101.
Faith, 253, 299; — compared with love, 1; — a development of the inner faculties, 121; — a spire, 256; — in Christ, 255.
Family, the first of churches, 180; — government of the, 262.
"Father, our," 132.
Faults, to look for, 143; — to tell friends of, 146.
Fear of God, 47; — as a motive, 68; — secretes acids, 80; — the influence of, 236.
Feeling is tropical, 27; — a torch, 55; — the bow, 67; — without speech, 148; — deeper than thought, 229.
Feelings, compared to a tree full of birds, 65; — like a river, 66; — exalted, not for daily life, 148; — compared to play of light and shade, 216.
Feminine traits, 218.
Ferry, swimming the, 284.
Field of battle, sight of a, 50.
Filial feeling towards God, 47.
Firefly, a, is not a star, 285.
Fishing, easiest with a short line, 104.
Flowers, 234; — supposition of their appearance before God, 111; — droop when filled with dew, 130; — in best clothes daily, 142; — why they receive the dew, 177; — dewdrops on, 180; — what they say to the night and to the morning, 266.
Foreign missions, 204.
Forgiveness, 158; — like a cancelled note, 108; — a hedgehog kind of, 128.
Foreordinations, 17.
Forest, the tumult of a, represented in Beethoven's symphonies, 82; — wind in the, 129; — men likened to the trees of a, 168; — play of light and shade in a, 216.
Foundation, Christ the, 125.
Foundations, care for the, 203.
Foundery, casting metal at a, 87.
Fountain, boring for a, 298.
Freedom, helping a slave to gain, 128.
Frescoed wall, the, 88.
Freshets likened to revivals, 34, 219.
Friend, to tell his faults to a, 146.
Frost, flowers cut by a single, 139.
Fruit, green, held tightly by the stem, 71; — bearing, the test of religion, 270.
Fruits, men should have their boughs full of, 13.
Future, the, likened to kaleidoscopic figures, 12; — the apprehensions of the, 171; — how to live for, 188.

Garden, the heart likened to a, 32; — despoiled by beasts, 50; — of the Lord, 51; — beauty of the word, 62; — how it gets a fountain, 298.
Gardens, men likened to, 199.
Generation, each, has its own light, 170
Generosity, fear of, by the selfish, 63.
Genius should not minister to self, 23.
Gift, ennobled by the giver, 155.
Glacier, flower under a, 127.
God, symbolized in nature, 4; — compared to the mother rocking the child, 5; — the noblest master in the arts, 14; — the bounty of, 24; — not supremely selfish, 26; — likened to the sun, 28; — gives freely, 30; —

pardons like a mother, 31; — embraces the names of father, mother, &c., 32; — the sustainer, 35; — multitudinous, 36; — represented under the form of a mountain, 47; — ploughs for us to plant, 54; — the smith, man the iron, 56; — may be approached in any sincere way, 79; — may be symbolized under different forms, 79; — not to be withstood, 95; — the countless mercies of, 97; — creation the relief of his fulness, 102; — receives the soul as the sea the bather, 103; — sin is a personal offence against, 103; — his care for all his work, 118; — the eternal *now*, 123; — not in a hurry, 134; — Christians to grow into the lineaments of, 136; — when terrible, 155; — comes in different garments, 169; — how manifest to us, 176; — high views of, 190; — all things obedient to, 198; — a parent, 199; — the boundless mercy of, 229; — "able to do abundantly," 231; — infinite in feeling, 231; — not vindictive, 232; — a God of love, 233; — only can satisfy with love, 239; — munificent, 243; — the draught master, 246; — affection towards, 255; — the gifts of, 255; — his agency in our troubles, 261; — the soul's need of, 284; — his law escaped out of Sunday, 286.

Gold, truth like, 242.

Goodness of God likened to a levee, 163.

Good will, the mother of the graces, 274.

Gospel to be preached first at home, 68.

Gospels, the, 137.

Grace, the heart of the flower, 70; — designed to develop man's nature, 112; — to carry men back to nature, 201.

Graces of slow growth, 32; — like Croton water, 105; — growth of, 176; — not sold as in an apothecary shop, 256; — likened to slides of a magic lantern, 295; — how wrought in the heart, 298.

Granary, a, 162.

Granite, hewing a block of, 100.

Grape vine in a flower pot, 142.

"Grass of the field," God's care for, the, 118.

Grasses, virtues like, 132.

Great men, 177.

Greatness, the way to, 38; — lies in the right using of strength, 52.

Growth, the mode of, 171.

Gulls, the flight of, 230.

Gun, an ill-loaded, 294.

Happiness not the chief end, 154, 175.

Hatred persistent and universal, 273.

Heart, the, compared to a dark cell, 36; — gifts of the, 76; — like a tropical plant, 140; — likened to a bud, 147; — its words of thanksgiving, 180; — the beating of a, 181; — subject to freshets, 194; — the yearning of the, 282; — knowledge, 224.

Hearts, the intents of, likened to flowers, 120; — like buds, 197; — like instruments, 207.

Heathenism, its respect for classes, 240; — likened to an undisturbed forest, 244; — the world hunting down, 245.

Heaven, 200, 257; — the realization of hope, 101; — seen as a landscape from a prison, 247; — the discoveries made in, 266; — the soul's welcome to, 294; — sweet to the fearful Christian, 296.

Hedgehog forgiveness, 128.

Helping word, a, 29.

Heresies, 205.

Heresy, hunters of, 53; — the greatest, 249.

Heroism, reasons for, 207.

Hinderances to grace, 21.

History of the world is all suffering, 44; — records only success, 90.

Hoarding, the impolicy of, 163.

Holy Spirit, aid of the, 173.

Home, piety at, 67; — not in a hotel, 142; — the centre of joy, 288.

Hope, 299; — compared with love, 1; — likened to a lantern, 28; — evan-

escent, 40; — an unfledged bird, 116; — excess of, 131; — base uses of, 268.
Horticulture, the author's experience in, 272.
Hospital, the world likened to a, 174; — illustration from a, 194.
Hotel, life in a, 142.
Hothouse plants, 59.
Hounds follow the scent while the dew is on, 49.
Household, a traitor to the, 45.
House of God, the, should be cheerful, 46.
House on the hill-top of cheerfulness, 288.
Human face, drawing the, 246.
Humboldt, 248.
Humboldt Glacier, the, 127.
Humiliations work out our joys, 58.
Hymn warbled by a child, 106.
Hymns, written in moments of rapture, 27; — and prayers, 167.
Hypocrites, 16.

Ideal, the, outlasts the real, 85.
Ill humor, 205.
Imagination, the true office of the, 96.
Improvements make new demands, 86.
India, war in, 245.
Infidelity of rich churches, 42.
Infidel philosophers, their views of the Bible, 225.
Insects, the annoyance of, 209.
Intellect kindled by emotion, 87; — the right use of, 114.
Institutions, old, compared to men made of the dust of mummies, 5; — not permanent, 62; — man more than, 136, 204.
Invisible things, the proof of, 252.
"Ism," definition of, 57.
Isthmus, how a route is found across the, 87.

Jacob, wrestling with God, 80.
Jacob's ladder, 173.
Japonica, the, 296.
Jeremiah, his immortality, 178.
Joy, like birds, 103; — a duty, 120, 162; — likened to music, 131.
Joys, often the shadows of sorrows, 21; — the hoarding of, 162.
Justice, to love, 167.

Kane, Dr., 127.
Kingdom of God within, 200.
Knowledge not from books, 224.

Landslides infrequent, 42.
Lantern, simile drawn from a, 28.
Latin, how learned, 260.
Law, every where resting upon man, 57; — sin not merely the breaking of, 103; — a rock smitten by Christ, for a river of love, 225; — of rewards and punishments, 289.
Laws, when not obligatory, 54; — like clocks, to be wound up, 129; — without public sentiment, 141; — when valuable, 206; — obsolete, likened to mummies, 239.
Laying on hands, 26.
Leaves, growth of, likened to the Christian life, 10; — talk of the, 147; — fall of the, 201.
Ledger, not the evidence of wealth, 77.
Lent, the passions never keep, 18.
Lettuce, chance sown, the best, 13.
Liberty, the chariot of, 28; — its defenders and propagators, 39; — Calvinism an aid to, 41; — is the soul's right to breathe, 70; — and equality, 169.
Lie, a, needs truth for a handle, 20.
Liebig, 248.
Life, 123; — its emotions and experiences the same in all ages, 6; — compared to a loom, 12; — a good, like a garden, 32; — its value and uses, 33; — to be loved, 41; — its proper end, 42; — as a river, 51; — as a voyage, 51; — compared to a man carrying a torch, 55; — compared to the making of a harp, 74; — unsatisfactory — good always in prospect, 74; — begins in the material, 94; — a web in the loom of time, 124; — the stream of, 146; — not left to our choice, 154; — composed of single feelings and actions, 158; — a voyage, 164; — present and future, 188; —

the end of, 192; — a frescoed chamber, 197; — a battle, 200; — its mingled joy and sorrow, 222; — a building, 227; — how to look at, 227; — the religious, 258; — a field, 292.
Life's ocean, buoys to be placed in, 55.
Life-preservers, 268.
Light, in our windows for travellers, 41; — to be reflected, 121.
Lights, in windows, the faculties likened to, 27; — in a village, 97.
Lighthouse, the intellect a, 114; — figure drawn from a, 163; — the church a, 277.
Lilies, in a New England lake, 73.
Limb, a broken, 156.
Line, to fish with a short, 104.
Locket worn by a soldier, 207.
Log, saturated, sinks in water, 237.
Logs floating down the Penobscot, 234.
Loom, breaking a thread in the, 14.
Loom of life, the, never stops, 12.
Loom of time, the, 124.
Longing for Christ, 249.
Lord's Prayer, the, 132.
Love, 299; — chief of the graces, 1; — compared to a cathedral tower, 1; — earthly, 34; — is God's loaf, 52; — like a seed from the tropics, 72; — in the heart, 94; — influence of, on the faculties, 105; — ownership, 149; — the central element, 163; — what is, 216; — the power to draw men to God, 233; — in few instances complete, 239; — the measure of Christian life, 241; — compared to a tide, 242; — more than justice, 294.
Love of God, the, 164.
Luther, greatest since his death, 178.
Luxuries, the love of, 179.

"Made," when a man is, 33.
Madrepores, destruction of piles by, 11.
Magnet, figure from the use of a, 116.
Maine, the lumberers in, 234.
Majority, one man in the right, is in the, 36.
Mammoth Cave of Kentucky, 280; — a child brought up in the, 213.
Man, a sword, 21; — should be like an orange tree, 39; — the iron, God the smith, 56; — surrounded by the pressure of responsibility, 57; — needs to go higher, when a, 66; — developed by overcoming evils, 68; — wrestling with fate, 80; — feeble in God's hands, 95; — God's creation, 137; — his first start, 143; — his obligation not dependent on the Bible, 149; — preventing the development of, 160; — likened to a ship, 168; — a name of power, 168; — his God-given right of liberty, 168; — evidence of the wickedness of, 190; — his escape from winter, 199; — needs a rough schoolmaster, 226; — preparation of the world for, 247; — wrecked like a ship, 284.
Manliness, the proper aim, 42.
Manly character, 218.
Manna, the fall of, 116.
"Marie Louise," the, 272.
Marriage, solemnity of, 180.
Marrow from his own bones, the student burns at night, 52.
Materialist, the, 252.
Meddler, religion a, 104.
Meekness, 158.
Memnon, the music of, 258.
Memory gleans, but renews not, 40.
Men, compared to vases, 15; — compared to trees, 37; — most vigilant, where there is least need, 63; — are tuned like violins, 66; — brothers at the judgment, 69; — carry signs of their life about them, 71; — remembered by their ideas, 85; — never stationary, 86; — in large business, likened to mountains, 92; — in large business likened to water-wheels, 92; — in the tide of vice powerless, 100; — hewn like granite, 100; — likened to different classes of flowers, 111; — rise upon their performances, 113; — rich and powerful, the duty of, 135; — likened to cathedrals, 162; — various like trees, 168; — like vines, 170; — distinctions among, 181; — likened to fenced gardens, 199; —

more than institutions, 204; — in prosperity like wheat with smut, 213; — drilled as in an army, 246; — reap what they have sown, 291.
Merchant, a Christian, 219; — the difference between a petty trader and a, 253.
Merchants, their interest in public conscience, 106.
Mercy of God, 97.
Michael Angelo, first sketches of, 14.
Military drill, 246.
Millennium, the world preparing for, 135.
Minds, likened to the Mammoth Cave, 280.
Ministers likened to surgeons, 156.
Mint, a true preacher is God's, 65.
Mirthfulness, the use of, 131.
Missionaries, the children of, 265.
Missions, the power of, 67.
Mississippi River, the, 291.
Mists rising from a valley, 140.
Moral nature, cultivation of the, 278.
Moralities insufficient for salvation, 13.
Morality contrasted with religion, 237; — must precede religion, 295.
Morning, our strength and spirits in the, 43; — the first hour of, 95.
Moses, his real life, 178.
Mother, God pardons like a, 31; — soothing a child, God like a, 78; — babe the anchor of the, 122; — of the author, her letters, 137.
Mother's heart, the, is the child's school room, 33; — bosom, the babe feeds on, 244.
Mountain top, view from a, 88.
Mountains, God likened to, 47; — the springs of the, 152.
Mozart, 158.
Munificence of God, 243.
Mummies, men made of the dust of, 5.
Musical instrument, the nature of men likened to a, 279.
Music in heaven, 19; — composed of single notes, 159; — earthly, 181; — if good, is sacred, 184; — every day a stroke of, 198; — loving like, 207; — the sweetest, 293.

National sins, 203.
Nations, the growth of, a charter of change, 28; — the hunting down of heathenism by the, 245.
Natural Bridge, the ascent of, 86.
Nature does not teach us how to die, 56; — and grace one, 70; — another Bible, 70; — physical, the source of our power, 75; — not destroyed by grace, 112; — full of symbols, 126; — its processes noiseless, 135; — the voice of, 179; — not oppugnant to grace, 201; — description of, in the Psalms, 220.
Needle, the, the devil's broadsword, 93.
Negative virtues, 182.
Negro, his skin the cause of his slavery, 165.
Nervousness, 191.
Nest, a last year's, 36.
New England boy, winter braved by a, 84.
New Testament, the beginning and end of the, 233.
New Testamentism, 42.
Nightingale, the, of the Psalms, 19; — his concern for criticism, 145.
Nightingales, a tree full, 65.
Nightingale's nest, quarrel over a, 217.
Night labor destroys the student, 52.
Nile, the line between the desert and the, 56.
Non-elect, the, 241.
Norway, midnight sun in, 98.
Nose, sect of the, 53.
Note, cancelled, an image of forgiveness, 108.

Oak, two feet high, 89; — two centuries old, its death the beginning of usefulness, 106; — growth of an, 226.
Obligations not upon Christians only, 157.
Ocean, evaporation of the, 226; — always the same, 283.
Ohio River, steamboat aground in the, 271.
Old Testament, 220.
Orange tree, 39.

Organ, the pulpit likened to the key-board of an, 274.
Outward acts, the power of, 114.

Paradoxes of truth, 108.
Parties to be used like railroad cars, 118.
Passions to be curbed, not exterminated, 75.
Past, right use of the, 123; — regrets of the, 171.
Patience, not learned from preaching, 61; — prayer for, 123.
Patriotism, made an argument for wrong, 135.
"Peace, be still," 106.
Peace of God, the, 77.
Penalties, 289.
Penance, 236.
Perfect, no man is, 124.
Perfection, through discipline, 68; — the doctrine of, 89.
Persecution, 262.
Perspiration and air curative, 40.
Pettifogging in one's own conscience, 36.
Petty cares, 42.
Phidias, the sculptor, 31.
Philosophy, 166.
Philosophers over a nightingale's nest, 217; — the rosy, 224.
Physical laws, the, 290.
Piano factory, life a, 154.
Picture of Christ in the gospel, 25.
Pictures in a magic lantern, 295.
Piety before theology, 2; — what is true, 172.
Pilgrim singing, the 23d Psalm compared to a, 9.
Pilot boats, 293.
Pine, the, on the mountain, 27.
Plans compared to green fruit, 71.
Plants, analogy drawn from the growth of, 48; — men compared to, 147; — hearts likened to, 195.
Plough overturning a cricket's nest, 160.
Ploughs, doctrines forged like, 186.
Plymouth Rock, the three strides towards, 38.
Poetry of the Bible, 220.
Politician, a, 254.
Politics, relation of religion to, 209.
Portrait of Washington, 165.
Porcelain, character likened to, 175.
Pot over a slow fire, 287.
Potato, its growth, 292.
Powers bring duties to their possessor, 37.
Praise, the interest on charity, 82.
Prayer, unwilling, 38; — when a test of piety, 121; — the Lord's, 132; — a shield, 227; — its unspoken aspirations, 230; — to boil over in, 287.
Prayers, smooth, 250.
Preach, what constitutes the right to, 26.
Preacher, a true, God's mint, 65.
Preaching, likened to a child plucking dewy grass, 35; — experimental, depth of, 63; — doctrine, 186.
Predestination, the doctrine of, 174.
Presbyterianism, a defender of liberty, 39.
Pride of men, the, 130; — when subdued, 134.
Principles only eternal, 85.
Prisons, the worst not of stone, 15.
Prisoners in castles, 247.
Progress, God's law, 68.
Promises compared to a highway to heaven, 30; — likened to cords reaching from heaven, 36; — of God, the, 110; — God abides by his, 208; — of God, like a boat to be rowed, 260.
Prophecy, the grandeur of, 88; — addressed to the imagination, 89.
Prosperity, influence of, 24; makes man a vortex, 60.
Protestantism, 38.
Proud men not grateful, 115.
Providence, the current for human plans, 128; — when men trust in, 160; — won't direct the ball, 193.
Psalm, twenty-third, the, 8; — seventy-third, like Beethoven's symphonies, 82.
Public opinion, 15; — compared to snow flakes, 17.
Public sentiment, 48, 204; — a battery, 192.
Public sins, 203.

Publican, prayer of the, 182.
Pulpit, the keyboard of an organ, 274.
Pump run down, 105.
Punishment of the wicked, 196 ; — inevitable, 289.
Puritans, the ideas of the, 40.
Puritanism, 42.
Purpose, man's, like a river, 137.
Pyramids, men likened to, 17 ; — the, 144.

Railroad train, the starting of a, 280.
Rainbows in the eyes, 94.
Rain drop, a, how it reaches the tree-top, 58.
Raphael, 31, 158 ; — the first sketches of, 14.
Reason, the use of, 252.
Refinement, excessive, 136, 218.
Refinements, the use of, 113.
Reform not always thorough, 251.
Reformers, 16 ; — always a hated race, 223.
Relations, not always of our blood, 69; — the good every where are, 133.
Religion desired by some as a lightning rod, 2 ; — not for Sunday only, 4 ; — sentimental and practical, 21 ; — the call to, 22 ; — the whole of life, 37 ; — a meddler, 104 ; — the four seasons of, not to be brought into one, 129 ; — the result of choice, 173 ; — its relations to politics, &c., 209 ; — greater than institutions, 225 ; — self-denial not characteristic of, 228 ; — contrasted with morality, 237 ; — the harmony of the faculties, 257 ; — desired as an insurance, 267 ; — a support to the soul, as a stake to a vine, 281 ; — separation of business from, 286 ; — the sum of the graces, 295 ; — the blossoming of the heart, 296.
Religious life, a river, 114 ; — a secret, 288.
Religious nature, the, 282.
Repentance, 236 ; — similes concerning, 102 ; — the experience of, not uniform, 110 ; — what is true, 117.
Republic, duty of citizens in a, 64.
Responsibility not divisible, 203.
Revenge, 206.
Reverence, 202.
Revivals, 188 ; — likened to freshets, 219, 234.
Rich, what it is to be, 77.
Riches, in giving up, 19.
Right, the triumph of, 169 ; — not enough to *desire* to be, 193.
River, peace likened unto a, 78 ; — the purpose likened to, 138 ; — Christian life, a new, 260.
Romans, the eighth chapter of, 210.
Rudder of the day, 95.
Ruin, the Bible a, 193.
"Ruined," when a man is, 34.
Rule, the purpose of, 206.
Russia moves southward, 245.

Sabbath a rock in the stream of time, 127 ; — the tide of the, 285.
Sabbaths should be hills of light, 84.
Sacred music, 184.
Sailors, 13.
Saint, a young, 294.
Saint John, the Gospel of, 137.
Samphire gatherers, simile drawn from, 35.
School, influence of the, 145.
Schools, driven westward, 272.
Sculpture, what is nobler than, 31.
Seasons, analogy drawn from the, 129 ; — men compared to plants in the several, 147.
Secrecy, use of, to the soul, 145.
Secret sins, 290.
Sects, undue prominence given to special doctrines by the, 53.
Self-conceit, 245.
Self-contemplation, 213.
Self-denial, 103, 228 ; — only one of the elements of religion, 12 ; — irksome to some professing Christians, 251.
Self-examination, 172, 251, 269, 271.
Self-isolation of genius, culpable, 23.
Self-respect, 92.
Self-restraint, 131.
Selfishness, 41, 140, 226 ; — not an attribute of God, 26 ; — of refinement

the, 136; — a worm at the root, 195; — a low country, 235.
Sentimental religion, 21.
Sermons, sound, 20; — labored, like wind over the sea, 106.
Shepherd, Christ the, 197.
Shield, a spear-dent in a, 44.
Ship, held by the anchor, likened to a soul anchored to secret sin, 11; — built of the old oak, 107; — engine to be bolted to the, 119; — how to prove the speed of a, 172; — unseaworthy, 192.
Ships, only the sails of, visible at a distance, 85; — meeting at sea, 217; — stranded, 284.
Shirking, by a fellow-laborer, 44.
Shower, singing likened to a, 29.
Sick, a physician needed by the, 259.
Sight, the pleasures of, 278.
Silkworm's web, 113.
Sin is against God, 103; — not divisible, 203; — punishment of, 289; — its inevitable consequences, 290.
Sincerity, in belief, not enough, 16; — in a preacher, 138.
Singing, feeling in, 29; — of a congregation, 129; — with prayer, 227.
Sinner, a, going to God, is never met with a scowl, 30; — true repentance of the, 183.
Sins, little, compared to madrepores, 11; — confession of, 23; — hide God's countenance, 44; — open and secret, 114.
Skim milk, to live, 64.
Slave, the duty of helping a, 128; — Bible or the, 184.
Slavery, 166, 204; — the abettors of, 28; — the kind of gospel which sanctions, 75.
Sleep, sacred, 143.
Smutting machines, 213.
Snow flakes likened to public opinion, 17.
Sobriety, what is meant by, 182.
Society, influence of public opinion on, 48; — requires new institutions, 62; — the growth of, 170.
Solstice, the winter, 261.
Soul, the, anchored to secret sin, 11; — likened to a house with apartments, 18; — the yearnings of, 67; — its life written upon the face of nature, 70; — loss of the, 127; — how it should go to God, 139; — its necessary secrecy, 145; — how God is made known to the, 176; — a bay filled by the tide, 242; — likened to a vine, 249; — likened to a house, 251; — likened to a bird, 255; — the response of the, compared to Memnon, 258; — its winter solstice, 261; — likened to a ship, 262; — clings like a vine, 281.
Soul-house, building a, 161.
Soul-structures, the rearing of, 102.
Spelling a syllable, 34.
Spheres, men have different, 134.
Spider's web, 113.
Springs in the mountains, 152.
Star, to make a, 277.
Stars, the, sparks from a forge, 102; — why they shine, 189; — the rays of, 194.
State, the pabulum of a, 173.
Statesman, a, 254.
Statue, the image of God likened to a, 3.
Steamboat aground in the Ohio River, 271.
Stoicism, 110.
Stream, damming a, 131.
Strong, duty of the, 171.
Students prefer night for labor, 52.
Success, 36; — is what history records, 90.
Successful man, the, 160.
Suffering is in all the history of the world, 44; — how borne, 109; — did not slip in at the fall, 109; — a part of God's plan, 191; — vicarious, 221; — not meritorious, 235.
Summer's morning, a, 256.
Sun, the, shines for all, 27; — at midnight in Norway, 98; — the sustainer of the system, 232.
Sunday, a sponge to wipe out the sins of the week, 4.
Sunday religion, 286.
Superciliousness, 202.

Swimmers, a rock in the mid-stream for, 127.
Swimming across East River, 284.
Switch on a railroad track, 29.
Sword, man likened to a, 21; — conscience likened to a, 29.
Symbols used by God, 66; — in a house, 124; — in nature, 126.
Sympathy, power of, 76.
Syro-Phœnician woman, the, 211.

Table, associations of the, 141.
Tear, a, used as a lens, 26.
Telescope, illustration from the, 26; — its lens, how dimmed, 43; — imagination like a, 96; — illustration from the use of a, 252.
Temptations without imply desires within, 73.
Texts likened to balls of twine, 211.
Thankful heart like a magnet, 116.
Thanks, the giving of, 115.
Theologians, their quarrels, 217.
Theology not the beginning of Christian life, 2.
Theatre, the, 251; — when a Christian should go to the, 139.
Thinking is creating, 228.
Thinker, a true, reports the discourse of God, 17.
Thought, exhaustless, 17; — the arrow, 67; — evil in, 115; — without speech, 148; — men of, 178; — rapid play of, 216; — deeper than speech, 229; — golden-orbed, 277.
Thoughts likened to a troop of birds, 50; — involuntary, 65.
Tide, love like a, 242.
Tides, the, 285.
Timber lodged in trees by freshets, 219.
Time ends not at once, 43.
Titian, duty of the pupil of, 275.
Tones, the seven, likened to the week, 43.
Torch, carrying in a windy street, a, 55.
Trades leave their mark upon the man, 71.
Train saved from destruction. 276.
Traitor, a fruit of what tree, 104.
Transfiguration, Raphael's picture of the, 270.
Traveller on a summer's morning, 257.
Tree, rain goes first to the roots of, 58; — how made to grow on the south side, 109; — the preacher likens himself to a, 150; — the fall of a, 289.
Tree of life, the, 152; — girdled, 167.
Trees grow tall and spindling in forests, 37; — tall, to shade the lower ones, 135; — old, the cutting down of, 151; — growing on the roots of old trunks, 179; — men likened to, 181; — without the garden, 215.
Trellis, the Bible a, 263.
Trial, the joy of victory over, 8.
Trials, the use of, 56; — like arrows from the bow of God, 195.
Trouble overwhelming, 80; — like a storm without, 81; — like deep water, 81; — to be braved like winter, 84.
Troubles caused by pride, 25; — some, how curable, 40; — small, 42; — victory over, 81; — God's tools, 100; — vanish like mists, 140; — the cure for, 202; — to be crossed over, 261.
Truth grows strong in defeat, 35; — doctrine, the skin of, 97; — the sphere of some to evolve, 134; — the currency of God, 144; — compared to clouds, &c., 166; — divine, never lost, 239; — likened to wheat from the tombs of Egypt, 240.
Truths developed for us as from eggs, 15.
Twine, the length of a ball of, 210.

Universalism, 233.

Vacation, death a, 189.
Vases, perfumed, 15.
Vegetation the great analogue, 48; — noiseless, 135.
Vengeance not a divine attribute, 232.
Vicarious suffering, 221.
Vices, frosted and ornamented, 129.
Vicious, longing for virtue by the, 100.
Village, lights by night in a, 97.

Vine, dialogue between a barren and a fruitful, 238 ; — examination of a, 269.
Vines, men like, 170 ; — their nature to cling, 280.
Violet, the, 28.
Violins out of tune, 223.
Violinist, the, screws up the key, 66.
Virtues in outline, 123 ; — few great, 132.
Voyage of life, the, 51, 164.

Wall Street, 165.
Warehouses, men likened to, 162
Washington, the portrait of, 164.
Watch, the examination of a, 268.
Water of life, the, 126.
Water-logged with anxiety, 237.
Waterwheel, the breaking of the, 92.
Way, Christ the, 93.
Wealth, and losses, 33 ; — the pursuit of, 144.
Weaving the web of life, 124.
Weeds, how destroyed, 176.
Wedding, the communion a, 202.
Week, the, likened to the seven tones, 43.
Wheat covered with smut, 212 ; — from the pyramids, 240 ; — best sown clean, 292.
" White robes," meaning of the, 122.
" Whosoever will," 234.
Wickedness of some persons, 192.
Window, the church likened to a, 32.
Windows, stained, 54.
Winter braved by a New England boy, 84 ; — wakening of earth from, 198.
Wisdom, the result of the past, 179.
Word of God, the, like a magic writing, 43.
Words, the bannerets of an army, 230.
Work, the best discipline, 73 ; — does not kill men, 80.
Women dependent on the needle, 93.
World, the, God's seed bed, 134 ; — fruitful, 169 ; — the misery of the, 174 ; — a hospital, 194 ; — God's cradle, 247.
Worlds, the creation of, 228.
Worry, the effect of, 80.
Worship, false idea of, 20.
Wreck of a great man, 284.
Wrestling with God, 80.

Yearnings of the soul, 67.
Young men, the conservative, 221.

LIFE THOUGHTS.

Now abideth these three: Faith, by which we see the glories of the eternal sphere; Hope, by which we mount towards them; and Love, by which we grasp and inherit them — therefore the greatest of these is Love.

Love, amid the other graces in this world, is like a cathedral tower, which begins on the earth, and, at first, is surrounded by the other parts of the structure. But, at length, rising above buttressed wall, and arch, and parapet, and pinnacle, it shoots spire-like many a foot right into the air, so high that the huge cross on its summit glows like a spark in the morning light, and shines like a star in the evening sky, when the rest of the pile is enveloped in darkness. So Love, here, is surrounded by the other graces, and divides the honors with them; but they will have felt the wrap of night and of darkness when *it* will shine, luminous, against the sky of eternity.

MANY men want wealth — not a competence alone, but a *five-story competence*. Every thing subserves this; and religion they would like as a sort of lightning rod to their houses, to ward off, by and by, the bolts of divine wrath.

THE way to begin a Christian life is not to study theology. Piety before theology. Right living will produce right thinking. Yet many men, when their consciences are aroused, run for catechisms, and commentaries, and systems. They do not mean to be shallow Christians. They intend to be thorough, if they enter upon the Christian life at all. Now, theologies are well in their place; but repentance and love must come before all other experiences. First a cure for your sin-sick soul, and then theologies. Suppose a man were taken with the cholera, and, instead of sending for a physician, he should send to a bookstore, and buy all the books which have been written on the human system, and, while the disease was working in his vitals, he should say, "I'll not put myself in the hands of any of these doctors. I shall probe this thing to the bottom."

Would it not be better for him first to be cured of the cholera?

THE Bible is the most betrashed book in the world. Coming to it through commentaries is much like looking at a landscape through garret windows, over which generations of unmolested spiders have spun their webs.

Our real commentators are our strongest traits of character; and we usually come out of the Bible with all those texts sticking to us which our idiosyncrasies attract.

IF one should send me from abroad a richly-carved and precious statue, and the careless drayman who tipped it upon the sidewalk before my door should give it such a blow that one of the boards of the box should be wrenched off, I should be frightened lest the hurt had penetrated farther, and wounded it within. But if, taking off the remaining boards, and the swathing bands of straw or cotton, the statue should come out fair and unharmed, I should not mind the box, but should cast it carelessly into the street.

Now, every man has committed to him a statue, moulded by the oldest master, not of Cupid, or Venus, or Psyche, or Jupiter, or Apollo, but the image of God; and he who is only solicitous for outward things, who is striving to protect merely the body from injuries and reverses, is letting the statue go rolling away into the gutter, while he is picking up the fragments and lamenting the ruin of the box.

A WEEK filled up with selfishness, and the Sabbath stuffed full of religious exercises, will make a good Pharisee, but a poor Christian. There are many persons who think Sunday is a sponge with which to wipe out the sins of the week. Now, God's altar stands from Sunday to Sunday, and the seventh day is no more for religion than any other. It is for rest. The whole seven are for religion, and one of them for rest.

ALL things in the natural world symbolize God, yet none of them speak of him but in broken and imperfect words. High above all he sits, sublimer than mountains, grander than storms, sweeter than blossoms and tender fruits, nobler than lords, truer than parents, more loving than lovers.

His feet tread the lowest places of the earth; but his head is above all glory, and every where he is supreme.

You might as well go to the catacombs of Egypt, and scrape up the dust of the mummies, and knead it into forms, and bake them in your oven, and call such things men, and present them, as citizens and teachers, for our regard, as to bring old, time-worn institutions to serve the growth and the living wants of to-day.

---

* What cares the child when the mother rocks it, though all storms beat without? So we, if God doth shield and tend us, shall be heedless of the tempests and blasts of life, blow they never so rudely.

Every man feels, and not strangely, that there never were such experiences of life as his own. No joy was ever like our joy, no sorrow ever like our sorrow. Indeed, there is a kind of indignation excited in us when one likens our grief to his own. The soul is jealous of its experiences, and does not like pride to be humbled by the thought that they are *common*. For, though we know that the world

* In church, one rainy Sabbath morning.

groans and travails in pain, and has done so for ages, yet a groan heard by our ear is a very different thing from a groan uttered by our mouth. The sorrows of other men seem to us like clouds of rain that empty themselves in the distance, and whose long-travelling thunder comes to us mellowed and subdued; but our own troubles are like a storm bursting right overhead, and sending down its bolts upon us with direct plunge.

But there have been human hearts, constituted just like ours, for six thousand years. The same stars rise and set upon this globe that rose upon the plains of Shinar or along the Egyptian Nile; and the same sorrows rise and set in every age. All that sickness can do, all that disappointment can effect, all that blighted love, disappointed ambition, thwarted hope, ever did, they do still. Not a tear is wrung from eyes now, that, for the same reason, has not been wept over and over again in long succession since the hour that the fated pair stepped from paradise, and gave their posterity to a world of sorrow and suffering. The head learns new things, but the heart forevermore practises old experiences. Therefore our life is but a new form of the way men have lived from the beginning.

When the landsman first goes down upon the deep, to see what storm-ploughing means, what furrows the wind draws, seedless and unplanted, he feels in every shivering nerve that never was such storm known before. Now, he bethinks himself with horror, there has come upon the deep a fury never till then let loose. But the clouds laugh, and the winds know, that ten thousand times before they have terrified just such inexperienced wretches. Yea, long ere a ship dared the central ocean, storms had navigated it, nor failed to pursue their dreadful sport ever since a keel crossed the perilous deep.

Not only are such experiences the hereditary legacy of men, rolled over and over, and sent down in succession upon every generation, but the methods by which men have met and conquered trouble, or been slain by it, are the same in every age. Some have floated on the sea, and trouble carried them on its surface as the sea carries cork. Some have sunk at once to the bottom as foundering ships sink. Some have run away from their own thoughts. Some have coiled themselves up into a stoical indifference. Some have braved the trouble, and defied it. Some have carried it as a tree does a wound, until by new wood it can overgrow and cover the old gash. A few in every age have known the divine art of carrying sorrow and trouble as wonderful food; as an invisible garment that clothed them with strength; as a mysterious joy, so that they suffered gladly, rejoicing in infirmity, and, holding up their heads with sacred presages whenever times were dark and troublous, let the light depart from their eyes, that they might by faith see nobler things than sight could reach.

The most affecting records of literature are those which repeat to us the sacred joy of souls in trial — their victory, and the causes of it. Job says, "Though He slay me, yet will I trust in him." Moses "endured as seeing Him who is invisible." Isaiah had sounded forth, "The wilderness and the solitary place shall be glad for them, and the desert shall rejoice and blossom as the rose. It shall blossom abundantly, and rejoice even with joy and singing; the glory of Lebanon shall be given unto it, the excellency of Carmel and Sharon; they shall see the glory of the Lord, and the excellency of our God. . . . And the ransomed of the Lord shall return and come to Zion with songs and everlasting joy upon their heads; they shall obtain joy and gladness, and sorrow and sighing shall flee away."

David has left no sweeter psalm than the short twenty-third. It is but a moment's opening of his soul; but — as when one, walking the winter street, sees the door opened for some one to enter, and the red light streams a moment forth, and the forms of gay children are running to greet the comer, and genial music sounds, though the door shuts and leaves the night black, yet it cannot shut back again all that the eye, the ear, the heart, and the imagination have seen — so in this psalm, though it is but a moment's opening of the soul, are emitted truths of peace and consolation that will never be absent from the world.

The twenty-third psalm is the nightingale of the psalms. It is small, of a homely feather, singing shyly out of obscurity; but, O, it has filled the air of the whole world with melodious joy, greater than the heart can conceive. Blessed be the day on which that psalm was born.

What would you say of a pilgrim commissioned of God to travel up and down the earth singing a strange melody, which, when one heard, caused him to forget whatever sorrow he had? And so the singing angel goes on his way through all lands, singing in the language of every nation, driving away trouble by the pulses of the air which his tongue moves with divine power. Behold just such an one! This pilgrim God has sent to speak in every language on the globe. It has charmed more griefs to rest than all the philosophy of the world. It has remanded to their dungeon more felon thoughts, more black doubts, more thieving sorrows, than there are sands on the sea shore. It has comforted the noble host of the poor. It has sung courage to the army of the disappointed. It has poured balm and consolation into the heart of the sick, of captives in dungeons, of widows in their pinching griefs, of orphans in their loneliness. Dying soldiers have died easier as it was read to them; ghastly hospitals have been illumined; it has visited the prisoner and broken his chains, and, like Peter's angel, led him forth in imagination, and sung him back to his home again. It has made the dying Christian slave freer than his master, and consoled those whom, dying, he left behind mourning, not so much that he was gone as because they were left behind, and could not go too. Nor is its work done. It will go singing to your children and my children, and to their children, through all the generations of time; nor will it fold its wings till the last pilgrim is safe, and time ended; and then it shall fly back to the bosom of God, whence it issued, and sound on, mingled with all those sounds of celestial joy which make heaven musical forever.

O IMPATIENT ones! Did the leaves say nothing to you as they murmured, when you came hither to-day? They were not created this spring, but months ago; and the summer just begun will fashion others for another year. At the bottom of every leaf stem is a cradle, and in it is an infant germ; and the winds will rock it, and the birds will sing to it all summer long, and next season it will unfold. So God is working for you, and carrying forward to the perfect development all the processes of your lives.

You have seen a ship out on the bay, swinging with the tide, and seeming as if it would follow it; and yet it cannot, for down beneath the water it is anchored. So many a soul sways towards heaven, but cannot ascend thither, because it is anchored to some secret sin.

Men, in their property, are afraid of conflagrations and lightning strokes; but if they were building a wharf in Panama, millions of teredos, so small that only the microscope could detect them, would begin to bore the piles down under the water. There would be neither noise nor foam; but in a little while, if a child did but touch the post, over it would fall as if a saw had cut it through.

Now, men think, with regard to their conduct, that, if they were to lift themselves up gigantically and commit some crashing sin, they should never be able to hold up their heads; but they will harbor in their souls little sins, which are piercing and eating them away to inevitable ruin.

"IF any man will come after me, let him deny himself, and take up his cross and follow me."

This is only one meaning of religion. If I should say of a garden, "It is a place fenced in," what idea would you have of its clusters of roses, and pyramids of honeysuckles, and beds of odorous flowers, and rows of blossoming shrubs and fruit-bearing trees? If I should say of a cathedral, "It is built of stone, cold stone," what idea would you have of its wondrous carvings, and its gorgeous openings for door and window, and its evanishing spire? Now, if you regard religion merely as self-denial, you stop at the fence, and see nothing of the pleasantness of the garden; you think only of the stone, and not of the marvellous beauty into which it is fashioned.

ONE might as well attempt to calculate mathematically the contingent forms of the tinkling bits of glass in a kaleidoscope as to look through the tube of the future and foretell its pattern.

WE sleep, but the loom of life never stops; and the pattern which was weaving when the sun went down is weaving when it comes up to-morrow.

MEN who neglect Christ, and try to win heaven through moralities, are like sailors at sea in a storm, who pull, some at the bowsprit and some at the mainmast, but never touch the helm.

OUR best actions are often those of which we are unconscious; but this can never be unless we are always yearning to do good.

In my garden at the West, I used sometimes to notice that the finest heads of lettuce were not in the beds, but on some southern ridge, where they had chanced to grow. It seemed as though random seeds always did the best, from a kind of wild emulation; but they never grew without the sowing, and the chance-sown seed was never wild.

If you shake the tree, you can bring down fruit, no doubt; but I remember, when a boy, the persuasion to get early out of bed was the thought of the large white apples that lay beneath the trees, awaiting the first comer — that had dropped upon the grass in the silent night, almost without a breath of wind to stir the branches. Now, I think every man ought to carry his boughs so full of fruits, that, like the apples which drop from silent dew, they will fall by the weight of their own ripeness for whoever needs to be refreshed. We should go home to the

2

threshing floor like a great harvest wagon full of sheaves, which at every jolt casts down ears for the gleaners, and stray seeds for the birds, and now and then a chance handful, which, blown by winds into nooks and corners, comes up to grow, and to bless another generation.

He who is false to present duty breaks a thread in the loom, and will find the flaw when he may have forgotten its cause.

When I was in the galleries of Oxford, I saw many of the designs of Raphael and Michael Angelo. I looked upon them with reverence, and took up such of them as I was permitted to touch as one would take up a love token. It seemed to me these sketches brought me nearer the great masters than their finished pictures could have done, because therein I saw the minds' processes as they were first born. They were the first salient points of the inspiration. Could I have brought them home with me, how rich I should have been! how envied for their possession! Now, there are open and free to us, every day of our lives, the designs of a greater than Raphael or Michael Angelo. God, of whom the noblest master is but a feeble imitator, is sketching and painting every hour the most wondrous pictures — not hoarded in any gallery, but spread in light and shadow round the whole earth, and glowing for us in the overhanging skies.

WHAT if the parent bird should sit, nervous and fluttering, upon the bough, when the young ones were hatching, and mourn because its beautiful egg shells were being broken?

Yet this is what we do. We have joys and truths deep as eternity, committed to us in the egg form, and the shell must needs be chipped before they can be born, and fly, full-fledged, singing, towards the gate of heaven. Yet we grieve and fear, and cling still to the undeveloped egg.

IF a man is odious in society, he might as well be in prison. The worst prisons are not of stone; they are of throbbing hearts, outraged by an infamous life.

THERE are many people in this world who are like perfumed vases from which the perfume has fled, all the surrounding objects attracting it; and so their life is not in *themselves*, but in their *things*.

It is often said it is no matter what a man believes if he is only sincere. This is true of all minor truths, and false of all truths whose nature it is to fashion a man's life. It will make no difference in a man's harvest whether he think turnips have more saccharine matter than potatoes — whether corn is better than wheat. But let the man sincerely believe that seed planted without ploughing is as good as with, that January is as favorable for seed sowing as April, and that cockle seed will produce as good a harvest as wheat, and will it make no difference? A child might as well think he could reverse that ponderous marine engine which, night and day, in calm and storm, ploughs its way across the deep, by sincerely taking hold of the paddle-wheel, as a man might think he could reverse the action of the elements of God's moral government through a misguided sincerity. They will roll over such an one, and whelm him in endless ruin.

They are not reformers who simply abhor evil. Such men become in the end abhorrent themselves.

Sometimes men who have been frankly wicked attempt to reform, and become locked-up hypocrites.

One man's heart beating against yours may be little to you; but when it is the echo of a thousand hearts, you cannot resist it. A single snow-flake,—who cares for it? But a whole day of snow-flakes, obliterating the landmarks, drifting over the doors, gathering upon the mountains to crash in avalanches,—who does not care for that? Private opinion is weak, but public opinion is almost omnipotent.

Some men are like pyramids, which are very broad where they touch the ground, but grow narrower as they reach the sky.

People say, "How fortunate it is that things have turned out just as they have—that I was prepared for this!" As if God did not arrange the whole! One might as well say, "How fortunate it is that I have a neck beneath my head, and shoulders under my neck!"

No man need fear that he will exhaust his substance of thought, if he will only draw his inspiration from actual human life. There the inexhaustible God pours depths and endless variety of truth; and the true thinker is but a short-hand writer endeavoring to report the discourse of God. Shall a child on the banks of the Amazon fear lest he should drink up the stream?

THERE are apartments in the soul which have a glorious out-look; from whose windows you can see across the river of death, and into the shining city beyond; but how often are these neglected for the lower ones, which have earthward-looking windows. There is the apartment of Veneration. Its ceilings are frescoed with angels, and all exquisite carvings adorn its walls; but spiders have covered the angel ceiling, and dust has settled on the delicate mouldings. The man does not abide there. The door of Conscience is rusted so it cannot be opened. Hope has but one downward-looking window, and Faith and Worship are cold and cheerless. All these are shut up in most soul-houses. In lower apartments you shall hear, in some riot and wassail, — for the passions never keep Lent, but are always holding Carnival, — and in others sighs and lamentations of wounded hopes, and in others the groanings of disappointed ambition, and in others bickerings and strifes, while in others there are sleep and stupidity.

Ah! most men live in these wretched apartments,

and never mount to those airy ones where they can hold commerce with God and angels. Now Christ comes to light up the house from foundation to roof-tree with the glory of God. He knocks at the door, and, when it is opened to him, he enters, and gives to every room order, and beauty, and the voice of song, and a wondrous fragrance from his robes, which have borrowed smell of every flower that grows in the celestial gardens. Who will open the door?

In this world, it is not what we *take* up, but what we *give* up, that makes us rich.

When a man unites with the church, he should not come saying, "I am so holy that I think I must go in among the saints," but, "O brethren, I find I am so weak and wicked that I cannot stand alone; so, if you can help me, open the door and let me enter."

Amid the discords of this life, it is blessed to think of heaven, where God draws after him an everlasting train of music; for all thoughts are harmonious and all feelings vocal, and so there is round about his feet eternal melody.

Many of our churches defy Protestantism. Grand cathedrals are they, which make us shiver as we enter them. The windows are so constructed as to exclude the light and inspire a religious awe. The walls are of stone, making us think of our last home. The ceilings are sombre, and the pews coffin-colored. Then the services are composed to these circumstances, and hushed music goes trembling along the aisles, and men move softly, and would on no account put on their hats before they reach the door; but when they do, they take a long breath, and have such a sense of relief to be in the free air, and comfort themselves with the thought that they have been good Christians!

Now, this idea of worship is narrow and false. The house of God should be a joyous place for the right use of all our faculties.

I had rather see a congregation laugh, when it is a sign of life in them, than to see them asleep under, appropriately called, sound sermons.

A lie always needs a truth for a handle to it, else the hand would cut itself which sought to drive it home upon another. The worst lies, therefore, are those whose blade is false, but whose handle is true.

THOSE who exalt sentimental religion, and ignore practical, ethical life, are like men who would improve ship architecture by cutting away the hull till it is no larger than a shingle, and spreading the sails till they are as big as the whole harbor. Every leaf must have a root which goes deep into the ground, and every sentimental blossom must have an ethical support.

IN this world, full often, our joys are only the tender shadows which our sorrows cast.

THE cares and infelicities of life, which are spoken of as "hinderances to grace," may be hinderances, but they are the only helps it has in this world. The voice of provocation is the voice of God calling us to the practice of patience.

A man in old age is like a sword in a shop window. Men that look upon the perfect blade do not imagine the process by which it was completed. Man is a sword. Daily life is the workshop, and God is the artificer, and those cares which beat him upon the anvil, and file his edge, and eat in, acid-like, the inscription upon his hilt, — these are the very things that fashion the man.

THE call to religion is not a call to be better than your fellows, but to be better than yourself. Religion is relative to the individual.

MANY professing Christians are like railroad station houses, and the wicked are whirled indifferently by them, and go on their way forgetting them; whereas they should be like switches, taking sinners off one track, and putting them on to another.

THERE ought to be such an atmosphere in every Christian church, that a man going there and sitting two hours should take the contagion of heaven, and carry home a fire to kindle the altar whence he came.

MANY persons come to the right point in conversion, but they never shove off. I question them about their state, and I find all as it should be; but they are waiting for something, they know not what — standing still in thought and feeling.

If you wind up the weights of a clock, and point the hands to the proper figures, and go away, you will find them in the same place when you return an hour after. Set it again, and an hour later it will be as you left it. What does it need? It needs to have the pendulum swing, and then it will keep time. Now, I am continually setting Christians; and when I look again, I find them just where I left them. What all such need is to swing the pendulum of active duties, and life expression of thoughts and feelings. Your hearts must be always ticking, if you would have them keep time with the sun of righteousness.

A MAN will confess sins in general; but those sins which he would not have his neighbor know for his right hand, which bow him down with shame like a wind-stricken bulrush, those he passes over in his prayer. Men are willing to be thought sinful in *disposition;* but in special *acts* they are disposed to praise themselves. They therefore confess their depravity and defend their conduct. They are wrong in general, but right in particular.

I THINK the wickedest people on earth are those who use a force of genius to make themselves selfish in the noblest things; keeping themselves aloof from the vulgar, and the ignorant, and the unknown; rising higher and higher in taste, till they sit, ice upon ice, on the mountain top of eternal congelation.

Now, as we ascend the hills of improvement, those who are poor and needy are not to hear our voices chanting ever farther and farther in the distance. No! by our singing we are to win others upward to the same heights to which we aspire.

THE superfluous blossoms on a fruit tree are meant to symbolize the large way in which God loves to do pleasant things.

WHEN my blood flows like wine, when all is ease and prosperity, when the sky is blue, and birds sing, and flowers blossom, and my life is an anthem moving in time and tune, — then this world's joy and affection suffice. But when a change comes, when I am weary and disappointed, when the skies lower into the sombre night, when there is no song of bird, and the perfume of flowers is but their dying breath, when all is sunsetting and autumn, then I yearn for Him who sits with the summer of love in his soul, and feel that all earthly affection is but a glow-worm light, compared to that which blazes with such effulgence in the heart of God.

I THINK half the troubles for which men go slouching in prayer to God are caused by their intolerable pride. Many of our cares are but a morbid way of looking at our privileges. We let our blessings get mouldy, and then call them curses.

IF you wished to look at a portrait of Raphael's, what would you think to see only the forehead uncovered, and then only the eyes, and so on, until all the features had been separately seen? Could you gain a true idea of the picture as a whole? Yet this is the way men look at the picture of Christ in the Gospels, reading a few verses and mottoes here and there, and never considering the life in its wholeness and harmony.

YOU are to accept as a Christian every one whose life and disposition are Christ-like, no matter how heretical the denomination may be to which he belongs.

Wherever you find faith, and righteousness, and love, and joy in the Holy Ghost, you are to look upon them as the stamped coin of Christ's kingdom, and as a legal tender from God to you.

I HAVE heard men teach that God has a right to glorify himself, and to appropriate every thing to his own delight — a doctrine which is shocking, and which represents him as living in almighty selfishness. Can we believe that he sits, self-poised, in eternity, admiring his own perfections and singing his own joys, when, against this, with regard to man, the whole Bible fulminates?

IT is neither the vote nor the laying on of hands that gives men the right to preach. One's own heart is authority. If one wishes to, and can, let him, though all church courts forbid. If he cannot preach to edification, he is not authorized, though all the ministers in Christendom ordain him. Any one who has a bell in him, that, ringing, will ring with "Holiness to the Lord," is a preacher.

ASTRONOMERS have built telescopes which can show myriads of stars unseen before; but when a man looks through a tear in his own eye, that is a lens which opens reaches in the unknown, and reveals orbs which no telescope, however skilfully constructed, could do; nay, which brings to view even the throne of God, and pierces that nebulous distance where are those eternal verities in which true life consists.

WHEN the church is cold and dead, those hymns which were written by God's saints in moments of rapture, seem extravagant, and we walk over them on dainty footsteps of taste; but let God's spirit come down upon our hearts, and they are as sweetness on our tongues; nay, all too poor and meagre for our emotions; for feeling is always tropical, and seeks the most intense and fervid expression.

GOING into a village at night, with the lights gleaming on each side of the street, in some houses they will be in the basement and nowhere else, and in others in the attic and nowhere else, and in others in some middle chamber; but in no house will every window gleam from top to bottom. So is it with men's faculties. Most of them are in darkness. One shines here, and another there; but there is no man whose soul is luminous throughout.

THE sun does not shine for a few trees and flowers, but for the wide world's joy. The lonely pine on the mountain top waves its sombre boughs and cries, " Thou art my sun." And the little meadow violet lifts its cup of blue, and whispers with its perfumed breath, " Thou art my sun." And the grain in a thousand fields rustles in the wind, and makes answer, " Thou art my sun."

So God sits, effulgent, in heaven, not for a favored few, but for the universe of life; and there is no creature so poor or so low that he may not look up with childlike confidence and say, " My Father! thou art mine."

THE man who carries a lantern in a dark night can have friends all around him, walking safely by the help of its rays, and he not defrauded. So he who has the God-given light of hope in his breast can help on many others in this world's darkness, not to his own loss, but to their precious gain.

THE abetters of slavery are weaving the thread in the loom, but God is adjusting the pattern. They are asses harnessed to the chariot of Liberty, and, whether they will or no, must draw it on.

THE fact that a nation is growing, is God's own charter of change.

YOU never can have congregational singing, if that is *all* you have. Unless you have singing in the family and singing in the house, singing in the shop and singing in the street, singing every where, until it becomes a habit, you never can have congregational singing. It will be like the cold drops, half water, half ice, which drip in March from some cleft of a rock, one drop here and another there; whereas it should be like the August shower, which comes ten million drops at once, and roars on the roof.

I like to see people sing when they have to stop in the middle of the verse and cry a little. I like such unwritten rests and pauses in the music.

When hymns come to the house of God all redolent of home associations, then singing will be what it ought to be — social Christian worship.

A HELPING word to one in trouble is often like a switch on a railroad track — but one inch between wreck and smooth-rolling prosperity.

MANY men carry their conscience like a drawn sword, cutting this way and that, in the world, but sheathe it, and keep it very soft and quiet, when it is turned within, thinking that a sword should not be allowed to cut its own scabbard.

EVERY loving word that God speaks to us acts back again, and makes music in his heart. He never says, with a scowl, "Here comes that poor, limping sinner again." The path of the sinner back to God is brighter and brighter all the way up to the smile of the face and the touch of the hand; and *that* is salvation.

GOD builds for every sinner, if he will but come back, a highway of golden promises from the depths of degradation and sin clear up to the Father's house.

NO experience will ever reveal to us what changes are yet to come to us, or what new growth or pruning we shall have.

We know not what a day will bring forth. We can become familiar with a landscape; we know where to find the waterfall and the shady ledge, where the violets grow in spring and the sassafras gives forth its odor; but we never can become familiar with our life-landscape; we never can tell where we shall come upon the shady dell, or where the fountains will gush and the birds sing. That is with God.

God pardons like a mother, who kisses the offence into everlasting forgetfulness.

Raphael did well, and Phidias did well; but it is not painter or sculptor who is making himself most nobly immortal. It is he who is making true impressions upon the mind of man; frescoes for eternity, that will not shine out till the light of heaven reveals them; sculptures, not wrought in outward things, but in the inward nature and character of the soul.

Our children that die young are like those spring bulbs which have their flowers prepared beforehand, and have nothing to do but to break ground, and blossom, and pass away. Thank God for spring flowers among men, as well as among the grasses of the field.

A Christianity which will not help those who are struggling from the bottom to the top of society needs another Christ to die for it.

Men plant prayers and endeavors, and go the next day looking to see if they have borne graces. Now, God does not send graces as he sends light and rain, but they are wrought in us through long days of discipline and growth. Acorns and graces sprout quickly, but grow long before ripening.

If any of you should die to-day, could you say to God, "Lord, here is my life work. Thou didst send me into life with a handful of seeds, and here is my heart, like a garden, full of flowers"?

The clearest window that ever was fashioned, if it is barred by spider's webs, and hung over with carcasses of insects, so that the sunlight has forgotten to find its way through, of what use can it be? Now, the church is God's window; and if it is so obscured by errors that its light is darkness, how great is that darkness!

If we are the Lord's, we need not fear to see our treasures disappear, to have the cradle become empty, and friend after friend fall away; for father, and mother, and brother, and sister, and husband,

and wife, and child are but sparks struck out from God — glowing names which, grouped together, mean God. So let us take our dear ones and enshrine them in him, and place them in that crystal sphere where loss can never come.

THE mother's heart is the child's school room.

WE are bound to be the almoners of God's bounty — not tax gatherers, to take away what little others have. As a father stands in the midst of his household, and says, "What is best for my children?" so we are to stand in the world, and say, "What is best for my brotherhood?"

WE say a man is "made." What do we mean? That he has got the control of his lower instincts, so that they are only fuel to his higher feelings, giving force to his nature? That his affections are like vines, sending out on all sides blossoms and clustering fruits? That his tastes are so cultivated that all beautiful things speak to him, and bring him their delights? That his understanding is opened, so that he walks through every hall of knowledge, and gathers its treasures? That his moral feelings are so developed and quickened, that he holds sweet commerce with Heaven? O, no — none of these things. He is cold and dead in heart, and mind, and soul. Only his passions are alive; but — he is worth five hundred thousand dollars!

And we say a man is "ruined." Are his wife and children dead? O, no. Have they had a quarrel, and are they separated from him? O, no. Has he lost his reputation through crime? No. Is his reason gone? O, no; it is as sound as ever. Is he struck through with disease? No. He has lost his property, and he is ruined. The *man* ruined! When shall we learn that "a man's life consisteth not in the abundance of the things which he possesseth"?

A MAN, in this world, is a boy spelling in short syllables; but he will combine them in the next.

EARTHLY love is a brief and penurious stream, which only flows in spring, with a long summer drought. The change from a burning desert, treeless, springless, drear, to green fields and blooming orchards in June, is slight in comparison with that from the desert of this world's affection to the garden of God, where there is perpetual, tropical luxuriance of blessed love.

DEFEAT is a school in which Truth always grows strong.

MY best presentations of the gospel to you are so incomplete! Sometimes, when I am alone, I have such sweet and rapturous visions of the love of God and the truths of his word, that I think, if I could speak to you then, I should move your hearts. I am like a child, who, walking forth some sunny summer's morning, sees grass and flower all shining with drops of dew. "O," he cries, "I'll carry these beautiful things to my mother." And, eagerly plucking them, the dew drops into his little palm, and all the charm is gone. There is but grass in his hand, and no longer pearls.

IN our own strength we can do nothing. Who is there that is not tired of climbing up the black face of the cliff of Resolution, to fall back again, day after day, upon the shore? They who gain their subsistence by searching for nests along dangerous heights search with their waists girdled with a cord let down from above, that, if they slip, they shall not fall and be lost. We need God's golden cords and bands of promises, reaching from heaven, to enable us to defy stumbling or downfall. "Cast down, but not destroyed."

SUCCESS is full of promise till men get it; and then it is a last year's nest, from which the bird has flown.

No man can go down into the dungeon of his experience, and hold the torch of God's word to all its dark chambers, and hidden cavities, and slimy recesses, and not come up with a shudder and a chill, and an earnest cry to God for divine mercy and cleansing.

THE most miserable pettifogging in the world is that of a man in the court of his own conscience.

A MAN in the right, with God on his side, is in the majority, though he be alone, for God is multitudinous above all populations of the earth.

Men think religion bears the same relation to life that flowers do to trees. The tree must grow through a long period before the blossoming time; so they think religion is to be a blossom just before death, to secure heaven. But the Bible represents religion, not as the latest fruit of life, but as the whole of it — beginning, middle, and end. It is simply *right living*.

Great powers and natural gifts do not bring privileges to their possessor, so much as they bring duties.

God designed men to grow as trees grow in open pastures, full-boughed all around; but men in society grow like trees in forests, tall and spindling, the lower ones overshadowed by the higher, with only a little branching, and that at the top. They borrow of each other the power to stand; and if the forest be cleared, and one be left alone, the first wind which comes uproots it.

We go to the grave of a friend, saying, "A man is dead;" but angels throng about him, saying, "A man is born."

The German Protestant declared, "I have rights as against the church." The Puritan Protestant declared, "I have rights as against government." The Independent or Congregational Protestant declared, "I have rights as against civil governments, church governments, and all mankind. Neither the multitudes nor the organized few can take from me what God gave, and I will preserve." These were the three great strides which landed on Plymouth Rock.

When your mind and heart are in such a state that praying is pushing a prayer through, like driving a wedge into a log, do you call it religion? It is as when your child, red-faced and choking with passion, is held up by the servant to kiss you. He comes because he is pushed; and do you call that love?

Whether they shall confess their faults or not, men generally leave to their moods, and not to their principles.

For four thousand years the strong had been rushing on in the road of privilege and power, seeking greatness. Christ stood in the path, and said, "Ye seek greatness. Ye are not even in the way to it. Ye are going up, but the way to greatness is down. Let him who would be great be the love-servant of all." Greatness consists in the facility and power of going down, and not in the facility of going up.

A MAN ought to carry himself in the world as an orange tree would if it could walk up and down in the garden — swinging perfume from every little censer it holds up to the air.

WHEREVER Presbyterianism has existed, it has always been found a strong defender of liberty. Wherever Congregationalism has existed, it has always been the propagator of liberty. The one builds granaries; and no rat nor mouse shall nibble the wheat there. The other throws the storehouse doors wide open, and saying, "The field is the world," it scatters the grain broadcast over the earth.

Presbyterianism has been a port in which liberty has taken refuge; a bulwark, behind which it has been protected. Congregationalism is an army, well equipped and disciplined, bearing right down on the enemy and taking possession of new territory.

How many hopes have quivered for us in past years — have flashed like harmless lightnings in summer nights, and died forever!

Memory can glean, but can never renew. It brings us joys faint as is the perfume of the flowers, faded and dried, of the summer that is gone.

The Puritan ideas were not seen to be of much value when they were first made known. They were like lands left by a father to infant children, which, when the children are of age, have become so valuable as to enrich them all. When the Puritan died, the property had not appreciated; but since then it has risen in value so that we have built this nation with it; and still it has not run out, at least in the northern part of the country.

There are many troubles which you cannot cure by the Bible and the Hymn Book, but which you can cure by a good perspiration and a breath of fresh air.

There is no system which equals Calvinism in intensifying to the last degree, ideas of moral excellence and purity of character. There never was a system since the world stood which puts upon man such motives to holiness, or which builds batteries that sweep the whole ground of sin with such horrible artillery. In its tendency to create strong individualism, which is the foundation of liberty, and to make men let each other alone, and say, "Stand back! the man is striving for his soul; put no obstacle in his way," — in both these directions Calvinism has always worked for liberty.

WE look down at our fellows as the eagle looks over the edge of the cliff at the mice which crawl so far below him. This is the selfishness of the moral nature. Our gifts and attainments are not only to be light and warmth in our own dwellings, but are as well to shine through the window, into the dark night, to guide and cheer bewildered travellers upon the road.

WE ought to love life; we ought to desire to live here so long as God ordains it; but let us not so encase ourselves in time that we cannot break the crust and begin to throw out shoots for the other life.

As it is only now and then that we have a landslide, while we are continually annoyed by the dust which sifts in at every crack, and door, and window, so it is only now and then that we have a crashing trouble, while we are perpetually annoyed by little daily cares and vexations.

Let it be understood that the end of our existence here is that we may be more God-like; and may we know that we shall become so by being more manly in the world, and that we are placed here to grow strong and noble, and not merely to enjoy.

The most dangerous infidelity of the day is the infidelity of rich and orthodox churches.

In the earlier ages of New England, the state was nothing but Congregationalism in civil affairs, and the church was nothing but republicanism carried into religious affairs. They reflected each other.

New Englandism is but another word for Puritanism in the Independent sense, and that is but another word for New Testamentism.

EVERY Saturday evening has to my ear a gentle knell. The week tolls itself away; the first, second, third, fourth, fifth, sixth, and the perfect seventh, and I can almost hear them beating a melodious measure as they recede.

Time does not end all at once. It is ending, in part, every day, and hour, and moment. And when the angel shall lift up his hand, and swear by Him who liveth forever that it shall be no longer, the years which are past will not then have ended more than now.

IN the morning, we carry the world, like Atlas; at noon, we stoop and bend beneath it; and at night, it crushes us flat to the ground.

GOD'S word is sometimes to us like a magic writing which has faded out and become invisible, and then, at other times, the lines reappear, and it flashes for us with a divine meaning.

YOU need not break the glasses of a telescope, or coat them over with paint, in order to prevent you from seeing through them. Just breathe upon them, and the dew of your breath will shut out all the stars. So it does not require great crimes to hide the light of God's countenance. Little faults can do it just as well. Take a shield, and cast a spear upon it, and it will leave in it one great dent. Prick it all over with a million little needle shafts, and they will take the polish from it far more than the piercing of the spear. So it is not so much the great sins which take the freshness from our consciences, as the numberless petty faults which we are all the while committing.

HISTORY is a mighty, thundering declaration of the falsity of the sentiment that God is not a God who will let men suffer. The history of the world is all suffering.

IF I am working beside a man, and I see that he tries to shirk and shift his labor upon me, I am angry with him. But if he says to me, "I am wounded, and cannot work," or, "I am lame," or "sick," then the thought comes to me at once, "You shall not work; I will help you." And so if a man says to us, "I know I did wrong; but I am weak. Blame me as little as you can, but help me as much as you can," that very confession disarms us, and we think better of him than we did before. Therefore it is that God so exhorts us to confess our sins to him. God is like us to this extent, that whatever in us is good is like God.

WHEN engineers would bridge a stream, they often carry over at first but a single cord. With that, next, they stretch a wire across. Then strand is added to strand until a foundation is laid for planks; and now the bold engineer finds safe footway, and walks from side to side. So God takes from us some golden-threaded pleasure, and stretches it hence into heaven. Then he takes a child, and then a friend. Thus he bridges death, and teaches the thoughts of the most timid to find their way hither and thither between the shores.

ANY feeling that takes a man away from his home, is a traitor to the household.

WHEN I see how much has been written of those who have lived; how the Greeks preserved every saying of Plato's; how Boswell followed Johnson, gathering up every leaf that fell from that rugged old oak, and pasting it away, — I almost regret that one of the disciples had not been a recording angel, to preserve the odor and richness of every word of Christ. When John says, "And there are also many other things which Jesus did, the which, if they should be written every one, I suppose that even the world itself could not contain the books that should be written," it affects me more profoundly than when I think of the destruction of the Alexandrian Library, or the perishing of Grecian art in Athens or Byzantium. The creations of Phidias were cold stone, overlaid by warm thought; but Christ described his own creations when he said, "The words that I speak unto you, they are life." The leaving out of these things from the New Testament, though divinely wise, seems, to my yearning, not so much the unaccomplishment of noble things, as the destruction of great treasures, which had already had oral life, but failed of incarnation in literature.

A CHURCH under the influence of veneration, merely, is a court house; and the judge sits there, and cold officers are standing by him, and men are waiting to receive their sentence. God's church is God's house; and God's house is our home; and a Christian home ought to be bright, cheerful, and happy. When God is the entertainer of his people, he thanks no man for "dim, religious light," or for casting forth the flowers, and extinguishing the lamps of hope and joy in the sanctuary.

THERE are two classes of people in the church: the religionists, who love God by trying to do right; and the Christians, who are inspired to do right by loving God.

WHEN once the filial feeling is breathed into the heart, the soul cannot be terrified by augustness, or justice, or any form of divine grandeur; for then, to such an one, all the attributes of God are but so many arms stretched abroad through the universe, to gather and to press to his bosom, those whom he loves. The greater he is, the gladder are we, so that he be our Father still.

But, if one consciously turns away from God, or fears him, the nobler and grander the representation be, the more terrible is his conception of the divine Adversary that frowns upon him. The God whom love beholds, rises upon the horizon like mountains which carry summer up their sides to the very top; but that sternly just God whom sinners fear, stands cold against the sky, like Mont

Blanc; and from his icy sides, the soul, quickly sliding, plunges headlong down to unrecalled destruction.

PUBLIC sentiment signifies the common march of good men's thoughts. It should be but a road, marked plain, that men may know the way to travel; but, instead of this, public sentiment is employed sometimes as a bribe to stop free thinking; as an intimidation to check free acting; as a bauble to lure approbativeness, or as a threatened fool's cap with which to terrify it. The virtues which public sentiment drills into cowards, may be of great benefit to society, but are of little credit to the men upon whom they are dragooned.

ALL human affairs follow nature's great analogue, the growth of vegetation. There are three periods of growth in every plant. The first, and slowest, is the invisible growth by the root; the second, and much accelerated, is the visible growth by the stem; but when root and stem have gathered their forces, there comes the third period, in which the plant quickly flashes into blossom and rushes into fruit.

The beginnings of moral enterprises in this world

are never to be measured by any apparent growth. The root is always concealed by the very soil which gives it life, and in which it spreads and hides. Then comes the middle period, in which it contends with opposing elements, but grows by the very things that would destroy it, as plants do by the winds that would prostrate them. At length comes the sudden ripeness and the full success, and he who is called in at the final moment deems this success his own. He is but the reaper, and not the laborer. Other men sowed and tilled, and he but enters into their labors. Before the time of Christ the world grew by the root; since that time until now it has grown by the stem; but ten thousand swelling buds of promise and of prophecy do now declare the time near at hand for flowers and fruits. Henceforth the world makes haste.

God washes the eyes by tears until they can behold the invisible land where tears shall come no more. O Love! O Affliction! Ye are the guides that show us the way through the great airy space where our loved ones walked; and, as hounds easily follow the scent before the dew be risen, so God teaches us, while yet our sorrow is wet, to follow on and find our dear ones in heaven.

THERE are some days when a man's thoughts seem to be as distinct from his personality as sparks are from the chimney of a winter's forge, streaming forth at night; or as birds are distinct from the trees from out of which they fly. Nor, if the mood be happy, are they indeed much unlike birds, when, in a feathery fury of delight, with a hundred songs of melodious dissonance, they sitting sing, and flying sing, and turn in the air with every fantastic gyration.

How sad is that field from which battle has just departed! By as much as the valley was exquisite in its loveliness, is it now sublimely sad in its desolation. Such to me is the Bible, when a fighting theologian has gone through it.

How wretched a spectacle is a garden into which cloven-footed beasts have entered! That which yesterday was fragrant, and shone all over with crowded beauty, is to-day rooted, despoiled, trampled and utterly devoured, and all over the ground you shall find but the rejected cuds of flowers, and leaves, and forms that have been champed for their juices and then rejected. Such to me is the Bible, when the pragmatic prophecy-monger and the swinish utilitarian have toothed its fruits and craunched its blossoms.

O garden of the Lord! whose seeds dropped down from heaven, and to whom angels bear watering dews night by night! O flowers and plants of righteousness! O sweet and holy fruits! we walk among you, and gaze with loving eyes, and rest under your odorous shadows; nor will we, with sacrilegious hand, tear you, that we may search the secret of your roots, nor spoil you, that we may know how such wondrous grace and goodness are evolved within you!

THE voyage of life should be right across the ocean, whose waters never shrink, and where the keel never rubs the bottom. But men are afraid to venture, and hang upon the coast, and explore lagoons, or swing at anchor in wind-sheltered bays. Some men put their keel into riches, some into sensuous pleasure, some into friendship, and all these are shallow for any thing that draws as deep as the human soul does. God's work in each age, indicated by the great movements of his providence, is the only thing deep enough for the heart. We ought to begin life as at the source of a river, growing deeper every league to the sea; whereas, in fact, thousands are like men who enter the mouths of rivers and sail upwards, finding less and less water every day; and in old age they lie shrunk and gaping upon dry gravel.

GREATNESS lies not in being strong, but in the right using of strength; and strength is not used rightly when it only serves to carry a man above his fellows for his own solitary glory. He is greatest whose strength carries up the most hearts by the attraction of his own.

THERE is a reason why students prefer the night to the day for their labors. Through the day their thoughts are diverted into a thousand streams; but at night they settle into pools, which, deep and undisturbed, reflect the stars. But night labor, in time, will destroy the student; for it is marrow from his own bones with which he fills his lamp.

LOVE is God's loaf; and this is that feeding for which we are taught to pray, "Give us this day our daily bread."

A CUNNING man overreaches no one half so much as himself.

God has appointed certain insects, birds, and beasts to be destroyers. They consume decaying matters; they roll up and feast on filth. To their palate life is unseasoned and insipid, but death has flavor. Such, also, are minor critics in literature, cynics in morals, and heresy-hunters in religion.

Sects and Christians that desire to be known by the undue prominence of some single feature of Christianity, are necessarily imperfect just in proportion to the distinctness of their peculiarities. The power of Christian truth is in its unity and symmetry, and not in the saliency or brilliancy of any of its special doctrines. If among painters of the human face and form there should spring up a sect of the eyes, and another sect of the nose, a sect of the hand, and a sect of the foot, and all of them should agree but in the one thing of forgetting that there was a living spirit behind the features more important than them all, they would too much resemble the schools and cliques of Christians, for the spirit of Christ is the great essential truth; doctrines are but the features of the face, and ordinances but the hands and feet.

It would almost seem as if there were a certain drollery of art which leads men who think they are doing one thing to do another and very different one. Thus men have set up in their painted church windows the symbolisms of virtues and graces, and the images of saints, and even of divinity itself. Yet now, what does the window do but mock the separations and proud isolations of Christian men? For there sit the audience, each one taking a separate color, and there are blue Christians and red Christians, there are yellow saints and orange saints, there are purple Christians and green Christians; but how few are simple, pure, white Christians, uniting all the cardinal graces, and proud, not of separate colors, but of the whole manhood of Christ!

WHEN laws, customs, or institutions cease to be beneficial to man, they cease to be obligatory.

THE strength of a man consists in finding out the way in which God is going, and going in that way too. For God goes before and ploughs, and we can but follow after and plant our seed in his furrow.

THE variableness of Christian moods is often a matter of great and unnecessary suffering; but

Christian life does not follow the changes of feeling. Our feelings are but the torch; and our life is the man that carries it. The wind that flares the flame does not make the man waver. The flame may sway hither and thither, but he holds his course straight on. Thus, oftentimes, it is, that our Christian hopes are carried as one carries a lighted candle through the windy street, that seems never to be so nearly blown out as when we step through the open door, and in a moment we are safe within. Our wind-blown feelings rise and fall through all our life, and the draught of death threatens quite to extinguish them; but, one moment more, and they shall rise and forever shine serenely in the unstormed air of heaven.

I THINK we ought to buoy for ourselves in our course, as we buoy a harbor. Off this shoal a black buoy floats, and says to those who sail by, as plainly as if it spoke in all languages, "Keep to the right here;" and over against it floats another, and says, "Keep to the left here." Now, in life's ocean, wherever we know the quicksands are, wherever we have once been stranded, let us sink the buoy and anchor of memory, and keep to the right or the left, as the shoal may be.

MANY pray to be made "men in Christ Jesus," and think in some miraculous way it will be given to them; but God says, "I will try my child, and see if he is sincere," and so he lays a burden upon him, and says, "Now stand up under it, for thus you are to grow strong." He sends a provocation, and says to him, "Be patient." He throws him into perplexities, and says, "Where now are thy resources?" If the ambitious ore dreads the furnace, the forge, the anvil, the rasp, and the file, it should never desire to be made a sword. Man is the iron, and God is the smith; and we are always either in the forge or on the anvil. God is shaping us for higher things.

THERE are some Christians whose secular life is an arid, worldly strife, and whose religion is but a turbid sentimentalism. Their life runs along that line where the overflow of the Nile meets the desert. It is the boundary line between sand and mud.

NATURE inspires us with a love of life, but can never teach us how to die. God would win us into death as the sun wins buds into blossoms. I often hear Christians speaking of a desire to die, that they may be free from the troubles of life; and they seem to me like birds that fly out of the tree frightedly, on account of noises which they hear beneath. But true Christians, it seems to me, should be like birds upon the sunset-top, stooping with half-opened wings, as if they heard the call of other birds in distant forests, and flew on purpose, and joyfully, to find their mates.

If you can find a place between the throne of God and the dust to which man's body crumbles where the focal responsibilities of law do not weigh upon him, I will find a vacuum in nature. They press upon him from God out of eternity, and from the earth out of nature, and from every department of life, as constant and all-surrounding as the pressure of the air.

There is a new word much used; it is *ism.* Every new or more perfect application of a Christian principle to the life of society, is called an ism, so long as men fight it, but a glorious evidence of the divinity of Christianity as soon as they are defeated by it. Selfish men abhor all isms of benevolence; proud men, all isms of condescension; the griping hand hates the open palm; greediness abhors moderation; and self-love thinks the love of others to be a spendthrift. And thus it comes to pass that *isms* are found and dreaded almost only among the great humanities of the day. If it be an ism to uplift the poor; to defend the slave; to maintain every where the right, though to do it overthrows time-honored institutions,—then God Almighty is the Father of isms, and has been propagating them since the world began; and he will lead the church from one ism to another, till it stands in Zion and before God.

What a pin is when the diamond has dropped from its setting, that is the Bible when its emotive truths have been taken away. What a babe's clothes are when the babe has slipped out of them into death, and the mother's arms clasp only raiment, would be the Bible, if the Babe of Bethlehem, and the truths of deep-heartedness that clothed his life, should slip out of it.

Our humiliations work out our most elevated joys. The way that a drop of rain comes to sing in the leaf that rustles in the top of the tree all summer long, is by going down to the roots first, and from thence ascending to the bough.

Many children grow up like plants under bell glasses. They are surrounded only by artificial and prepared influences. They are house-bred, room-bred, nurse-bred, mother-bred — every thing but *self-bred.* The object of training is to teach the child to take care of himself; but many parents use their children only as a kind of spool on which to reel off their own experience; and they are bound and corded until they perish by inanity, or break all bonds and cords, and rush to ruin by reaction.

We have the promises of God as thick as daisies in summer meadows, that death, which men most fear, shall be to us the most blessed of experiences, if we trust in him. Death is unclasping; joy, breaking out in the desert; the heart, come to its blossoming time! Do we call it dying when the bud bursts into flower?

Men who stand on any other foundation than the rock Christ Jesus are like birds that build in trees by the side of rivers. The bird sings in the branches, and the river sings below, but all the while the waters are undermining the soil about the roots, till, in some unsuspected hour, the tree falls with a crash into the stream; and then its nest is sunk, its home is gone, and the bird is a wanderer. But birds that hide their young in the clefts of the rock are undisturbed, and, after every winter, coming again, they find their nests awaiting them, and all their life long brood the summer in the same places, impregnable to time or storm.

It is one of the worst effects of prosperity to make a man a vortex instead of a fountain; so that, instead of throwing out, he learns only to draw in.

In the first years of a church, its members are willing to endure hardships and to make great exertions; but when once it is prosperous, they desire to take their ease; as one who builds a ship is willing to work all the way from keel to deck, until she is launched; thenceforward, he expects the ocean to buoy him up, and the winds to bear him on. The youth-time of churches produces enterprise; their age, indolence. But even this might be borne, did not these dead men sit in the door of their sepulchres, crying out against every living man who refuses to wear the livery of death. I am almost tempted to think that if, with the end of every pastorate, the church itself were disbanded and destroyed, to be gathered again by the succeeding teacher, we should thus secure an immortality of youth.

THERE is no such thing as preaching patience into people, unless the sermon is so long that they have to practise it while they hear. No man can learn patience except by going out into the hurly-burly world, and taking life just as it blows. Patience is but lying to, and riding out the gale.

As musicians sometimes go through perplexing mazes of discord in order to come to the inexpressible sweetness of after chords, so men's discords of trouble and chromatic jars, if God be their leader, are only preparing for a resolution into such harmonious strains as could never have been raised except upon such undertones. Most persons are more anxious to stop their sorrow than to carry it forward to its choral outburst. "Now, no chastening for the present seemeth to be joyous, but grievous; nevertheless, *afterward*, it yieldeth the peaceable fruits of righteousness unto them that are exercised thereby."

It is sometimes of God's mercy that men in the eager pursuit of worldly aggrandizement are baffled; for they are very like a train going down an inclined plane — putting on the brake is not pleasant, but it keeps the car on the track.

To the end of the world the word *garden* shall be sweeter than flower or fruit could make it; for the Son of God, the fairest thing that ever grew, was planted there, and sprang from thence in celestial bloom and glory.

Men often think an institution to *be* good because it has *done* good; but institutions are often only another kind of national school book, whose object it is to help the scholar to pass on and leave *it* behind. Neither boys nor society are to be kept forever in the hornbook. There must be, in any healthful society, a process of absorption, or of reconstruction of its organizations. Principles never change; their incarnations continually do. A society whose institutions are unchanging is itself ungrowing. The living body alters. Only the dead rest. That is a brave and good institution which speedily digs its own grave.

When our cup runs over, we let others drink the drops that fall, but not a drop from within the rim, and call it charity; when the crumbs are swept from our table, we think it generous to let the dogs eat them; as if that were charity which permits others to have what we cannot keep; which says to Ruth, "Glean after the young men," but forgets to say to the young men, "Let fall also some of the handfuls of purpose for her."

There is no such preaching as the experience which a man gives who has just realized the sinfulness of his soul. I often hear myself out-preached by some new convert who can hardly put words together. Some say experimental preaching is shallow. Shallow! It is deep as the soul of God.

Men are afraid of breaking down where they are strongest, but are seldom afraid of their weaknesses. If a man is hard, he fears mellowness. A proud man watches lest he should let himself down. A selfish man is vigilant against being unduly tempted by profuse kindness; and no man has a more salutary fear of rash generosity than he whose pores are sealed so tight that all the suns of prosperity cannot open them. Men are apt to guard themselves where it is impossible for them to be overcome; but they are quite careless of those open avenues through which temptation comes and goes so easily that they are unconscious of wrong doing because they are not pained by it.

It is not well for a man to pray, cream; and live, skim milk.

Some men say, to retire to a little blissful nook, with a few congenial ones to love, and to hear the distant roaring of life as those in forests hear the ocean, — the music, and not the storm, — would be all the happiness they would ask on earth. Now, where society is but a grand machine of despotism, where all civil affairs are put away from the citizen, and all religious affairs are in the hands of the official priest, so that it is treason to be active in politics, and sacrilege to be freely active in religion, then retirement and leisure may be as virtuous as they are safe. But in our land, where society is an unbounded field for individual exertion of every kind, and a man's usefulness is limited only by his own original power, one needs a special edict of Providence to justify him in retiring from life.

When leisure is a selfish luxury, its very activity, when it stirs, is apt to be only a kind of indolence taking exercise, that it may the better digest its selfishness.

EVER since the time of Christ, the divine Helmsman has been steering the world straight towards the lighthouse of Love.

A TRUE preacher is God's mint. God heats his heart till the truth flows like molten gold, and his utterance is prepared, as dies are, to stamp on the coin what God has cut in him. But thousands of preachers are only exchange brokers, who run between bank and customer to carry old coin back and forth for commercial uses. There is need for these too, only lower down.

A MAN might as well fill a tree full of nightingales, and, standing on the ground, attempt to control their notes and to hold them enchoired together, as to attempt to control by his volitions the multiplied thoughts and feelings of his own soul. Some persons hearing this will say, "A man can regulate his mind as easily as his house." Certainly, if he has nothing more in his mind than is in his house; but faculties ought not to be furniture. We can appoint the bounds and the directions of our thoughts and feelings, but within those bounds we can no more control their individual spring, than a man can control all the motions of the drops of water in a stream, because he has the power to fix its shores.

MEN think God is destroying them because he is tuning them. The violinist screws up the key till the tense cord sounds the concert pitch; but it is not to break it, but to use it tunefully, that he stretches the string upon the musical rack.

THERE is always the need for a man to go higher, if he has the capacity to go.

THERE is no food for soul or body which God has not symbolized. He is light for the eye, sound for the ear, bread for food, wine for weariness, peace for trouble. Every faculty of the soul, if it would but open its door, might see Christ standing over against it, and silently asking by his smile, "Shall I come in unto thee?" But men open the door and look down, not up, and thus see him not. So it is that men sigh on, not knowing what the soul wants, but only that it needs something. Our yearnings are homesicknesses for heaven; our sighings are for God, just as children that cry themselves asleep away from home, and sob in their slumber, know not that they sob for their parents. The soul's inarticulate moanings are the affections yearning for the Infinite, and having no one to tell them what it is that ails them.

THERE is much contention among men whether thought or feeling is the better; but feeling is the bow, and thought the arrow, and every good archer must have both. Alone, one is as helpless as the other. The head gives artillery, the heart, powder. The one aims and the other fires.

SPREADING Christianity abroad is sometimes an excuse for not having it at home. A man may cut grafts from his tree till the tree itself has no top left with which to bear fruit. In the end, the power of Christian missions will be measured by the zeal of enlightened piety at home, as the circulation of blood at the extremities of the body will depend upon the soundness of the lungs and heart. I do not say that we should not send the gospel abroad; but that we may do it, there must be more of it at home. We must deepen the wells of salvation, or drawing will run them dry.

Many men affect to despise fear, and in preaching resent any appeal to it; but not to fear where there is occasion, is as great a weakness as to fear unduly, without reason. God planted fear in the soul as truly as he planted hope or courage. Fear is a kind of bell, or gong, which rings the mind into quick life and avoidance upon the approach of danger. It is the soul's signal for rallying.

The world never was so low as at the creation. There is never so little of a tree as when it is in the seed. The births of God Almighty are births of weakness. Every thing in the universe comes to its perfection by drill and marching — the seed, the insect, the animal, the man, the spiritual man. God created man at the lowest point, and put him into a world where almost nothing would be done for him, and almost every thing should tempt him to do for himself. The very help which God gives men, is by teaching them how to help themselves. Want, sorrow, mistake, and all that men call evils, are but disciplinarians, who insist that the scholar shall learn his lesson himself, and who punish him until he does.

LOOK not alone for your relations in your own house or in your own sphere. The blood of Christ is stronger for relationship than blood of father or mother. Look above you. All there are yours. Go down even to the bottom of society. All below you are judgment-day brothers; and God's eternity is on them and you alike.

How wonderful is what we call association! I hang some thought upon an object, and say, "Whenever I come hither, ring for me as a bell of joy;" and upon another I fasten an experience, saying to it, "Toll to me of sadness;" and to another, "Give forth some bold, inspiring strain;" and to another, "Speak to me always of hope." And, thereafter, each thing, true to its nature, whether it be tree, or place, or rock, or house, or that which is therein, never forgets its lesson. Yea, and when we forget, they make us to remember, singing to us the notes which we had taught them. Thus the heart, though it may not dismember itself, to give a soul to the material world, has yet a power half to create in physical things a soul in each for itself. So its life is written out, and it keeps a journal upon trees, upon hills, upon the face of heaven. Is it not for this, then, that in turn God has used every object in nature, every event in life, every function of society, every affection and endearment of human love, yea, and things that are not, the very silences of the world, and memories that are but disembodied events, to represent to us by association his nature and affections? Thus the heaven and the earth do speak of God, and the great natural world is but another Bible, which clasps and binds the written one; for nature and grace are one. Grace is the heart of the flower, and nature but its surrounding petals.

LIBERTY is the soul's right to breathe, and when it cannot take a long breath, laws are girdled too tight. Without liberty man is in a syncope.

THAT which the persecutors once said of the apostles, ought still to be said of every Christian man: "And they took knowledge of them, that they had been with Jesus." Acts iv. 13.

Men carry unconscious signs of their life about them. Those that come from the forge, and those from the lime and mortar, and those from the humid soil, and those from dusty travel, bear signs of being workmen, and of their work. One need not ask a merry face or a sad one whether it hath come forth from joy or from grief. Tears and laughter tell their own story. Should one come home with fruit, we say, "Thou art come from the orchard;" if with hands full of wild flowers, "Thou art from the fields;" if one's garments smell of mingled odors, we say, "Thou hast walked in a garden." But how much more, if one hath seen God, hath held converse of hope and love, and hath walked in heaven, should he carry in his eye, his words, and his perfumed raiment, the sacred tokens of divine intercourse!

When the fruit is yet green, the stem holds tightly to the bough; but when it is ripe, it falls with the first wind. So hold on tightly to your plans in life until God shows you that they are ripe — that they have accomplished their purpose; and then let them go; let them go without a murmur.

LOVE, in this world, is like a seed taken from the tropics, and planted where the winter comes too soon; and it cannot spread itself in flower-clusters and wide-twining vines, so that the whole air is filled with the perfume thereof. But there is to be another summer for it yet. Care for the root now, and God will care for the top by and by.

I HEARD a man who had failed in business, and whose furniture was sold at auction, say that when the cradle, and the crib, and the piano went, tears would come, and he had to leave the house to be a man. Now, there are thousands of men who have lost their pianos, but who have found better music in the sound of their children's voices and footsteps going cheerfully down with them to poverty, than any harmony of chorded instruments. O, how blessed is bankruptcy when it saves a man's children! I see many men who are bringing up their children as I should bring up mine, if, when they were ten years old, I should lay them on a dissecting table and cut the sinews of their arms and legs, so that they could neither walk nor use their hands, but only sit still and be fed. Thus rich men put the knife of indolence and luxury to their children's energies, and they grow up fatted, lazy calves, fitted for nothing, at twenty-five, but to drink deep and squander wide; and the father must be a slave all his life, in order to make beasts of his children. How blessed, then, is the stroke of disaster which sets the children free, and gives them over to the hard but kind bosom of Poverty, who says to them, "Work!" and, working, makes them men!

LIKE those fair New England lakes, greened around with meadows, of translucent depth and silver sand, on whose surface armies of white lilies, golden-crowned, unfold to the sun, so the Christian's heart should be. All its feelings and affections should open into life like those white lilies, and deep amid the blossom petals should be seen the golden crown of love.

TEMPTATIONS are enemies outside the castle seeking entrance. If there be no false retainer within, who holds treacherous parley, there can scarcely be even an offer. No one would make overtures to a bolted door or a dead wall. It is some face at the window that invites proffer. The violence of temptation addressed to us is only another way of expressing the violence of the desire within us. It costs nothing to reject what we do not wish, and the struggle required to overcome temptation measures the strength in us of the temptible element. Men ought not to say, "How powerfully the devil tempts!" but, "How strongly I am tempted!"

To be weighed down with a sense of our own incompleteness; to long for that which we have not and cannot gain; to descry noble attainments, as islands in the sea, eagerly sought, but which change to clouds as we draw near; to spend our life in searching for the hidden land, as Columbus for the new continent, and to find only weeds floating, or a broken branch, or, at best, a bird that comes to us from the unknown shore; this it is to be on earth — to live. And yet, are not these very yearnings the winds which God sends to fill our sails and give us good voyage homeward?

It is not so much by the symmetry of what we attain in this life that we are to be made happy, as by the enlivening hope of what we shall reach in the world to come. While a man is stringing a harp, he tries the strings, not for music, but for construction. When it is finished it shall be played for melodies. God is fashioning the human heart for future joy. He only sounds a string here and there to see how far his work has progressed.

THAT gospel which sanctions ignorance and oppression for three millions of men, what fruit or flower has it to shake down for the healing of the nations? It is cursed in its own roots, and blasted in its own boughs.

MEN utter a vast amount of slander against their physical nature, and attempt to repair deficient virtue by maiming their animal passions. These are to be trained, guided, restrained, but never crucified or exterminated, for they are the soil in which we were planted. Our life on earth begins in the body, and depends for vigor upon the fulness and power of our physical nature. An acorn at first sprouts from the soil, and spreads its young leaves upon the surface of the ground. Every year its top grows away from it towards heaven; yet the top neither forgets nor scorns the earth-buried root. The brightest leaf which the sun loves, or the wind waves on the topmost bough, has leave to be beautiful by what the root gives it, and carries in its veins the blood which the cold root sucked up from the moist earth. The top will famish when the root is hungry.

The way to avoid evil is not by maiming our passions, but by compelling them to yield their vigor to our moral nature. Thus they become, as in the ancient fable, the harnessed steeds which bear the chariot of the sun.

HAPPY is the man who has that in his soul which acts upon the dejected as April airs upon violet roots. Gifts from the hand are silver and gold, but the heart gives that which neither silver nor gold can buy. To be full of goodness, full of cheerfulness, full of sympathy, full of helpful hope, causes a man to carry blessings of which he is himself as unconscious as a lamp is of its own shining. Such an one moves on human life as stars move on dark seas to bewildered mariners; as the sun wheels, bringing all the seasons with him from the south.

MEN long for Christ on earth. Christ in heaven is not only faint and dim, but they think a heavenly Being cannot have earthly love. There may be more purity, they think, in heavenly love than in earthly, but less heartiness, and heartiness is what they long for. Now Christ returned to heaven that he might love more, not less. This was a part of the glory which he had laid aside and was to take again. On earth his soul stood but in the bud. He went to a fairer clime that he might blossom, and now the heavens and the earth are full of the fragrance of his love. Incarnation was limitation. Ascension was expansion. There was not room enough for such a heart while in the body. It came as a seed, and grew, but we saw only the sprouting and the leaves. Death ripened it back again to the golden fulness of a heavenly state.

No man can tell whether he is rich or poor by turning to his ledger. It is the heart that makes a man rich. He is rich or poor according to what he *is*, not according to what he *has*.

God says the peace of the man who loves him shall flow like a river; * and if ours is not such, it is because its springs are not in Mount Zion — because its sources are the marshes and the low-

* "O that thou hadst hearkened to my commandments! then had thy peace been as a river, and thy righteousness as the waves of the sea." Isaiah xlviii. 18.

lands, and not the crystal fountains of the hills. This peace shall not be like a shower, falling with temporary abundance, but like the river which flows by the cottage door, always full and always singing. The man hears it when he rises in the morning; he hears it in the quiet noon; he hears it when the sun goes down; and if he wakes in the night, its sound is in his ear. It was there when he was a child; it was there when he grew up to manhood; it was there when he was an old man; it will murmur by his grave upon its banks, and sing and flow for his children after him. It is to such a river that God likens the divine bounty of peace given to his people.

How little do we know of this peace of God! We deem ourselves happy if we have one serene hour out of the twenty-four; and if now and then there comes a Sabbath which is balm at morning, and sweetness through the still noon, and benediction at evening, we count it a rare and blessed experience.

The child frightened in his play runs to seek his mother. She takes him upon her lap, and presses his head to her bosom; and with tenderest words of love she looks down upon him, and smooths his hair, and kisses his cheek, and wipes away his tears. And then, in a low and gentle voice, she sings some sweet descant, some lullaby of love, and the fear fades out from his face, and a smile of satisfaction plays over it, and at length his eyes close, and he sleeps in the deep depths and delights of peace. God Almighty is the mother, and the soul is the tired child; and he folds it in his arms, and dispels its fears, and lulls it to repose, saying, "Sleep, my darling; sleep. It is I who watch thee." "He giveth his beloved sleep." The mother's arms encircle but one; but God clasps every yearning soul to his bosom, and gives to it the peace which passeth understanding, beyond the reach of care or storm.

A MAN has a right to picture God according to his need, whatever it be. This being shut up by ecclesiasticism to a narrow way of coming to God has stifled many a soul. The whole round of symbols has been employed to represent God to us, the loftiest as well as the lowest things. The bird that fans the sun, and the bird that hides from it under the leaf, are alike taken to symbolize Jehovah.

A man has a right to go to God by any way which is true to him. If you can think it out, that is your privilege. If you can feel it out, that is your privilege. One thing is certain: the child has a right to nestle in his father's bosom, whether he climbs there upon his knee or by the chair from behind; any way, so that it is his father. Wherever you have seen God pass, mark it, and go and sit in that window again.

It is not work that kills men; it is worry. Work is healthy; you can hardly put more upon a man than he can bear. Worry is rust upon the blade. It is not the revolution that destroys the machinery, but the friction. Fear secretes acids; but love and trust are sweet juices.

Men who have always thrust obstacles aside come to think their power invincible, and to make themselves a battering ram against fate and circumstances. And when God comes down to oppose them, at first they try to wrestle with him; but they limp all their life after, like Jacob of old, for God never wrestles with a man without throwing him.

There are four degrees in men's experience of trouble. The lowest, and most pitiable, is that in which trouble overwhelms a man; in which he is carried away by the force and swell of its waves, as a leaf is borne down the current of a rushing river. Shame that a man, — a *man*, — the son of God, and the heir of immortality, should be so swept and swayed by circumstances — a little money more or a little less — should crouch and fall down, unable to rise. May God spare me from seeing any of you in such a case. The second degree is that in which the man's troubles are about him like deep waters, but do not quite overpower him. He is just able to stand, and to keep his head above the waves. This is better than the first, but is the lowest of all that deserves the name of good. The third degree is that in which the man's heart is like a room where the father sits with his family, while the storm roars without. The floods beat against the windows; the wind whistles and moans at every crevice; but he heeds it not, for the fire burns brightly, and his wife and children sit smiling in its glow. Here the man has so far conquered his trials that he has peace within. The fourth, and highest, degree is that in which the man's troubles have become luminous to him, in which he is victorious over them, and makes them yield him strength and joy. And it is God's design, in wrestling with men, to bring them to this state, in which their griefs shall be the food of ecstasy and the wine of triumph.

To be praised, and to have the reputation of liberality, is the way many people have of taking interest on what they lend to the Lord. It is probable that benevolence is only the cat's paw of vanity, when our obscure and casual kindnesses seem to us like pale, inodorous flowers grown in a solitary wood, and only public and bruited charities have color and fragrance. A man should fear, when he enjoys only what good he does publicly. Is it not the publicity, rather than the charity, that he loves? Is it not vanity, rather than benevolence, that gives such charities? A man must be very rich in secret charities before he can bear the strain of public beneficence.

THE seventy-third psalm reminds me of some of Beethoven's symphonies; and *these*, again, always make me think of the tumult of the forest, when the wind roars and swells and surges with wild discord among the trees; when the branches creak and crash against each other, and every bough has a separate wail. By and by the wind lulls; and when twilight is beneath, and all the forest is quiet, or only so much noiseful as the insects make it, then some bird on a tree-top sings out clear and sweet, and his song goes floating away over the wood, the very soul of peaceful joy. And it seems to me that the symphonies of Beethoven — that Milton of musicians — reproduce in themselves the sounds of the forest. In the opening passages, the half-concordant discords clash one upon another; there is moaning, and strife, and war of sound; but, at length, out of the jar and the conflict is evolved a clear-flowing melody, as sweet as the song of the bird, and as gentle as the twilight rustle of the leaves.

Now, this psalm is like the symphonies; for its opening verses clash upon each other, and are full of tumult and yearning.

"But as for me, my feet were almost gone, my steps had well nigh slipped. For I was envious at the foolish when I saw the prosperity of the wicked. For there are no bands in their death, but their strength is firm. They are not in trouble as other men; neither are they plagued like other men. . . . Verily, I have cleansed my heart in vain, and washed my hands in innocency. For all the day long have I been plagued, and chastened every morning."

But when this strain is ended, then rises the sweet and joyful descant, "Nevertheless, I am continually with thee; thou hast holden me by my right hand. Thou shalt guide me by thy counsel, and afterward receive me to glory. Whom have I in heaven but thee? and there is none upon earth that I desire besides thee. My flesh and my heart faileth; but God is the strength of my heart, and my portion forever."

Through the week we go down into the valleys of care and shadow. Our Sabbaths should be hills of light and joy in God's presence; and so, as time rolls by, we shall go on from mountain top to mountain top, till at last we catch the glory of the gate, and enter in to go no more out forever.

We should brave trouble as the New England boy braves winter. The school is a mile away over the snowy hill, yet he lingers not by the fire; but, with his books slung over his shoulder, and his cap tied closely under his chin, he sets out to face the storm. And when he reaches the topmost ridge, where the powdered snow lies in drifts, and the north wind comes keen and biting, does he shrink and cower down beneath the fences, or run into the nearest house to warm himself? No; he buttons up his coat, and rejoices to defy the blast, and tosses the snow wreaths with his foot; and so, erect and fearless, with strong heart and ruddy cheek, he goes on to his place at school.

Now, when the fierce winds of adversity blow over you, and your life's summer lies buried beneath frost and snow, do not linger inactive, or sink cowardly down by the way, or turn aside from your course for momentary warmth and shelter, but, with stout heart and firm step, go forward in God's strength to vanquish trouble, and to bid defiance to disaster. If there is ever a time to be ambitious, it is not when ambition is easy, but when it is hard. Fight in darkness; fight when you are down; die hard, and you won't die at all. That gelatinous-bodied man, whose bones are not even muscles, and whose muscles are pulp, — that man is a coward.

THE things which most concerned men in past ages — food, raiment, wealth, place, personal honor — are all forgotten now; but those things which seemed to them the most shadowy and unsubstantial, — their faith, their ideals, their principles, — these are now the only abiding remembrancers. Thus men are kept alive on earth by that which is invisible, and sunk to the bottom by that which is material. Time is made up of waters so thin, that nothing may float thereon which is heavier than unseen truths and heart treasures. As, at sea, we descry ships by the sails which lift themselves high above the curve of the ocean, while the dark and heavy hulls, where the freights are, are sunk below the sight; — so, the convoys of men that sailed in the past are no longer seen where they carried the much-prized freight, but in the lifting up of their spars and sails against the heaven, high above the bend and curve of the ocean of time.

THE more thorough a man's education is, the more he yearns for and is pushed forward to new achievement. The better a man is in this world, the better he is compelled to be. That bold youth who climbed up the Natural Bridge, in Virginia, and carved his name higher than any other, found, when he had done so, that it was impossible for him to descend, and that his only alternative was to go on and scale the height, and find safety at the top. Thus it is with all climbing in this life. There is no going down. It is climbing or falling. Every upward step makes another needful; and so we must go on until we reach heaven, the summit of the aspirations of time.

WHENEVER an emotion rises up and projects its life into the intellect, and the intellect is magnetized by it, the truths belonging to that emotion will be clearer seen under these vision-judgments than at any other time. Many men confound moral excitements with those of their passions, and think it not prudent to act upon their feelings. They wait till excitement has cooled. The excitement of passion should cool, but of the nobler powers, never. I should as soon think of saying to the workmen at a foundery, "Why do you pour that liquid, scintillating iron into the mould? Why do you not wait till it is cold before you do it?" as of asking a man why he heeded his convictions, and his judgments of moral truths, when his intellect was roused and his heart on fire. If he waits till he has cooled down, they will be as dross and cinders compared to what they would have been when his heart throbbed and was alive with blessed excitement.

An exploring party are seeking the best route across the isthmus for a canal from ocean to ocean. The country is unknown to them, and they make but little progress in their search. At length the leader descries a mountain, misty blue, against the horizon, and knows that its top will show them the whole way on either side. So on they press, now fording streams, and now lost in the obscurity of forests, but ever keeping the mountain before them, and drawing nearer and nearer, till, at nightfall, they rest upon its base, and with the morning light climb its side, and, lo! the land lies, picture-like, below them, stretching away on either hand to both oceans. They mark the watercourses, and the trend of the valleys, and behold, to the west, how the mountains open like a gate to the Pacific Sea, and how, to the east, a broad river with unconscious skill finds its way through the lowlands to the Atlantic. But suppose, while they can thus easily determine their course, some conservative among them should exclaim, "This is all folly. If we would judge rightly, we must be down where the valleys curve and the rivers run," and, heeding his advice, they should all descend the mountain. Would they find their way, down there? Would not the jungle shut them in, and hide from them the whole map?

Now, the soul's hours of strong excitement are its luminous hours — its mountains of vision, from which it looks over the landscape of life with unobstructed gaze. And the observations it then takes, and the judgments it forms, as far transcend the scope and truth of its ordinary sight and reasoning as the view from the seaward-looking mountain transcends the view from the pent-up valley.

I AM profoundly affected by the grandeur of prophecy. God unveils the frescoed wall of the future, not so much that we may count the figures, and measure the robes, and analyze the pigments, but that, gazing upon it, our imaginations may be enkindled, and hope be inspired, to bear us through the dismal barrenness of the present. Prophecy was not addressed to the reason, nor to the statistical faculty, but to the imagination ; and I should as soon think of measuring love by the scales of commerce, or of admiring flowers by the rule of feet and inches, or of applying arithmetic to taste and enthusiasm, as calculations and figures to these grand evanishing signals which God waves in the future only to tell the world which way it is to march.

THE disputes which have filled the church upon the doctrine of perfection seem to me to have been pitiable. They reveal the narrowest conception of human character. God's idea of perfection is not mere conformity to rule and law, but, with this, development into a state far beyond any thing known among men. Perfection is ripeness ; but time is not a summer long enough to ripen the soul. Heaven is the soul's summer.

The perfection of the schools is a kind of mandarin perfection. Suppose a Chinese mandarin, whose garden was filled with dwarfed plants and trees, should show me an oak tree, two feet high, growing in a pot of earth, and should say to me, —

" A perfect tree must be sound at the root — must it not ? And it must have all its branches complete, and its leaves green. Look here. This root is sound; there is no decay in the trunk; it has the full number of branches; the leaves are bright and green, and little acorns are ripening all over it. It is a perfect tree; why do you not admire it?"

A miserable two-foot oak! I turn from it to think of God's oak in the open pasture, a hundred feet high, wide-boughed, and braving the storm.

Now, when a man comes to me talking of perfection, and says, "A perfect man must have such and such qualities — must he not? He must control his passions and appetites, and regulate his affections. He must not sin in this thing, or that thing, or the other. Such am I. I do not commit this fault, or fall into that error. I have trained and schooled myself. Behold me! I am perfect!" I can but exclaim, "Miserable two-foot Christian!" I have no patience with this low standard, these earthly comparisons, this relative goodness. I must outgrow this pot of earth. God's eternity is in my soul, and I shall need it all, to grow up to the measure of the stature of the fulness of Christ.

Not that which men do worthily, but that which they do successfully, is what history makes haste to record.

DUST, by its own nature, can rise only so far above the road; and birds which fly higher never have it upon their wings. So the heart that knows how to fly high enough, escapes those little cares and vexations which brood upon the earth, but cannot rise above it into that purer air.

WHEN mists have hung low over the hills, and the day has been dark with intermittent showers, at length, great clouds begin to hurry across the sky, the wind rises, and the rain comes pouring down; then we look out and exclaim, "Why, this is the clearing-up shower." And when the floods have spent themselves, the clouds part to let the blue sky tremble through them, and the west wind bears them away seaward, and, though they are yet black and threatening, we see their silver edges as they pass, and know that just behind them are singing birds and glittering dew drops; and, lo! while yet we look, the sun bursts forth, and lights them up in the eastern heaven with the glory of the rainbow.

Now, to the Christian whose life has been dark with brooding cares that would not lift themselves, and on whom chilling rains of sorrow have fallen at intervals through all his years, death, with its sudden blast and storm, is but the clearing-up shower; and just behind it are the songs of angels, and the serenity and glory of heaven.

THE truest self-respect is not to think of self.

MEN in extensive and prosperous business are often a target for envy to shoot at; and when they fail and go down, there are thousands who wickedly rejoice in their fall. But in our days some men are institutions. They do not stand like Pompey's Pillar or Cleopatra's Needle, towering to the sky, detached and alone; they are like mountains which carry forests far up their sides, and shelter and nourish ten thousand living things in their shadow. Some one says, "Why do you care that that water wheel is broken? A black, lumbering thing, half of the time in the water and half of the time out. Why do you not care for the nicer wheels and spindles within the building?"

I do care, and therefore I am sorry for the breaking of the great wheel. Its axis passes within, and by drum and bands its power is communicated to the various rooms, and every spindle is dependent upon its revolutions. When an earthquake comes, by as much as a house is elevated above the others, by so much is its ruin greater than theirs — the third story crashing into the second, and the second into the first. Now, men in extensive business are mountains of shelter; ponderous wheels that turn the mill; lofty houses which cannot fall without causing wide-spread disaster; and when we hear of their failure, we must not think of them alone, but also of the ten thousand dependants who are affiliated with them. In a not irreverent sense it may be said, they are "set for the fall and rising of many in Israel."

"I AM the way." As a road is that along which men go to their daily avocations, God chooses it to represent himself in this universal use, this underlying support of all things. Who would dare to say this of God but God? Some beasts carry their young, and some birds carry their young, and mothers carry their children; but who but God could say, "I am the road; press me with your feet." This is the highway cast up; and on it the ransomed of the Lord shall return and come to Zion, with songs and everlasting joy upon their heads.

I PITY those women whose staff is their needle; for when they lean upon it, it pierces, not their side, but their heart. The devil's broadsword, in this world, has often been the needle with which a woman sews to earn her daily bread. I think the needle has slain more than the sword of war.

When there is love in the heart, there are rainbows in the eyes, which cover every black cloud with gorgeous hues.

Our life begins in the senses. Men walk upon the ground; but above it God has sprung the blue arch of heaven, and they live by breathing the air. So it is with our interior life. The material world is the foundation, the grand workshop for our faculties; but if this be all, — if there hangs not above it God's invisible realm of truth, in which we breathe, — there can be no healthy living. That a plant may grow, we put manure into the soil; but when the roots have taken hold upon it, and it has shot up into stem, and leaves, and flowers, we do not pour manure into the white blossom. It holds up its cup, and says, "O Heaven! send thy light, and drop down thy dew." And the light glows, and the dew falls, and the flower expands by feeding upon the air.

So man's life must begin in the material. He

must first learn how to live as an animal, and must employ all those forces which will contribute to his development; but when he comes to the blossoms of faith, and hope, and courage, he needs other aliment. They must unfold, and be nourished in God's upper air.

Let the day have a blessed baptism by giving your first waking thoughts into the bosom of God. The first hour of the morning is the rudder of the day.

When God shakes men as dust from under the summer threshing-floor, the right hand of a man's strength is as powerless as the left hand of a man's weakness, and his wisdom is as folly. What avails the wisdom of the apple to make it cling to the bough when it is ripe in autumn time? or the wisdom of the leaf to hold it fast to the stem when the tempest calls? or the wisdom of the tree to make it stand secure when a rock from the cliff comes crashing down through its piny branches? When God sends storms upon men, they must imitate the humble grass, which saves itself by lying down. It is better to lie down than to break down. Therefore it is said, "Humble yourselves before the mighty hand of God, that in due season he may raise you up."

When at last the sound of death shall be in our ears, may it be but the noise of the wheels of God Almighty's chariot come to take us home — our schooling over, and our long vacation begun in heaven. Forever! Not this side the grave, which extinguishes all, but in that proud land which lies beyond, unseen by mortal eye, thank God! and unwet by mortal tear.

That which men suppose the imagination to be, and to do, is often frivolous enough and mischievous enough; but that which God meant it to be in the mental economy is not merely noble, but supereminent. It is the distinguishing element in all refinement. It is the secret and marrow of civilization. It is the very eye of faith. The soul without imagination is what an observatory would be without a telescope.

As the imagination is set to look into the invisible and immaterial, it seems to attract something of their vitality; and though it can give nothing to the body to redeem it from years, it can give to the soul that freshness of youth in old age which is even more beautiful than youth in the young. It always seems to me that, before we leave this realm, deep affections take hold of the life to come by the hands of ideality, so that this quality in the old, hovers upon the edge and bound of life, the morning star of immortality. Thus it is with men as with evening villages. The lights in some dwellings are extinguished soon after twilight; in others, they hold till nine o'clock; one by one they go out, until midnight; but a few houses there are where the student's lamp or lover's watching torch holds bright till morning pours their light into the ocean of its own. So such men bring through the flooded hours of darkness the light of yesterday into to-day, and are never dark and never die. Thus it comes to pass as it is written, "Upon those who sat in the region and shadow of death a great light is arisen."

DOCTRINE is nothing but the skin of Truth set up and stuffed.

So many are God's kindnesses to us, that, as drops of water, they run together; and it is not until we are borne up by the multitude of them, as by streams in deep channels, that we recognize them as coming from him. We have walked amid his mercies as in a forest where we are tangled among ten thousand growths, and touched on every hand by leaves and buds which we notice not. We cannot recall all the things he has done for us. They are so many that they must needs crowd upon each other, until they go down behind the horizon of memory like full hemispheres of stars that move in multitudes and sink, not separate and distinguishable, but multitudinous, each casting light into the other, and so clouding each other by common brightness.

THERE are moral crises in life — certain conjunctures of affairs when God displays himself as he never does at other times; and if we do not then make observations, like some stellar phenomena, certain truths will not come again for ages, and to us, never!

Suppose a man had travelled weary miles northward to see the midnight sun, and at length he reaches the little village in Norway where astronomers say at twelve o'clock the sun will touch the horizon, and then begin to ascend. He looks at his watch, and sees that it is ten o'clock, and says, "Some time yet. I am tired. I'll rest a while." And so he throws himself down, and is soon lost in slumber. Meanwhile the sun descends, till, at the appointed time, his lower limb rests upon the pines that skirt the horizon; and then he slowly rises again into the great round of heaven. By and by the man awakes, and looks at his watch, and finds that it is two o'clock. The sun is two hours high; he has missed the very thing which he journeyed so far to see, and, having but a single day, must needs depart as he came.

Now, there are men who pray for clearer views of God, for a greater nearness to him, for an opener heaven and more resplendent hope. At length, God, who loves to come in storms, draws near to them. Their sorrow, their trouble, their confusion of affairs, the darkness about them, are clouds which bring God upon their bosom. In that solemn eclipse, hid behind trouble, God would have taught an open ear some things which the whole life had pined to know. He would have shown them time, men, affairs, the glory of the world, as they see them who in heaven stand at God's right hand. But men are so absorbed in their trials that they neither hear nor see. The disciples lost the solemn passion of Christ through sleep; and, until now, sleep or tears have hid from men those very truths which would have given everlasting wakefulness to the soul, and wiped all sad weeping from the eyes. No men have need to be so vigilant, so attentive, so listening, so appreciative, as those who are in deep trouble. Sorrow is Mount Sinai. If one will go up and talk with God, face to face, he must not fear the voice of thunder, nor the trumpet sounding long and loud.

One of the affecting features in a life of vice is the longing, wistful outlooks given by the wretches who struggle with unbridled passions, towards virtues which are no longer within their reach. Men in the tide of vice are sometimes like the poor creatures swept down the stream of mighty rivers, who see people safe on shore, and trees, and flowers, as they go quickly past; and all things that are desirable gleam upon them for a moment to heighten their trouble, and to aggravate their swift-coming destruction.

Troubles are often the tools by which God fashions us for better things. Far up the mountain side lies a block of granite, and says to itself, "How happy am I in my serenity — above the winds, above the trees, almost above the flight of the birds! Here I rest, age after age, and nothing disturbs me."

Yet what is it? It is only a bare block of granite, jutting out of the cliff, and its happiness is the happiness of death.

By and by comes the miner, and with strong and repeated strokes he drills a hole in its top, and the rock says, "What does this mean?" Then the black powder is poured in, and with a blast that makes the mountain echo, the block is blown asunder, and goes crashing down into the valley. "Ah!" it exclaims as it falls, "why this rending?" Then come saws to cut and fashion it; and humbled now, and willing to be nothing, it is borne away from the mountain and conveyed to the city. Now it is chiselled and polished, till, at length, finished in beauty, by block and tackle it is raised, with mighty hoistings, high in air, to be the top-stone on some monument of the country's glory.

So God Almighty casts a man down when he wants to chisel him, and the chiselling is always to make him something finer and better than he was before.

It is a joy to know that there is a realm where all those aspirations which have beckoned us only to crown us still with thorns, shall be realized; and where there is no bud which shall not burst into blossom, and no blossom which shall fall without being filled into fruit.

Like those airy sprites in fairy tales who rear the building through the night, unseen in the process, but clear and distinct in the morning's completion, so years, and hours, and moments are silently rearing, in this world's darkness, a soul-structure whose proportions the sunlight of eternity shall reveal.

God made the world to relieve an over-full creative thought; as musicians sing, as we talk, as artists sketch when full of suggestions. What profusion is there in his work! When trees blossom there is not a single breastpin, but a whole bosom full of gems; and of leaves they have so many suits that they can throw them away to the winds all summer long. What unnumbered cathedrals has He reared in the forest shades, vast and grand, full of curious carvings, and haunted evermore by tremulous music; and in the heavens above, how do stars seem to have flown out of his hand, faster than sparks out of a mighty forge!

When a man undertakes to repent towards his fellow-men, it is repenting straight up a precipice; when he repents towards law, it is repenting into the crocodile's jaws; when he repents towards public sentiment, it is throwing himself into a thicket of brambles and thorns; but when he repents towards God, he repents towards all love and delicacy. God receives the soul as the sea the bather, to return it again, purer and whiter than He took it.

EVERY Christian should begin to doubt himself, if he finds, after ten years, that self-denial is as hard in the same things as it was at first.

THERE are joys which long to be ours. God sends ten thousand truths, which come about us like birds seeking inlet; but we are shut up to them, and so they bring us nothing, but sit and sing a while upon the roof and then fly away.

WHEN a man defrauds you in weight, he sins against *you*, not against the scales, which are only the instrument of determining true and false weight. When men sin, it is against God, and not against his law, which is but the indicator of right and wrong. You care little for sins against God's law. It has no blood in its veins, no sensibility. Now, every sin that you commit is personal to God, and not merely an infraction of his *law*. It is casting javelins and arrows of base desire into His loving bosom. I think no truth can be discovered which would be so powerful upon the moral sense of men, as that which should disclose to them that sinning is always a personal offence against a personal God. Law without, is only an echo of God's heart-beat within.

PAUL and his companions meddled, to be sure, only with the religion of Jesus Christ; but that, faithfully preached, meddles with every thing else on earth.

A TRAITOR is good fruit to hang from the boughs of the tree of liberty.

WHEN I used to fish in mountain streams, if I had a short line and rod, I could direct it easily, and throw it into this or that pool as I pleased; but if I let out my line till it was twenty or thirty feet long, I could not direct it, but I was the victim of every floating stick, and jutting rock, and overhanging bough. So I have seen men wading down the stream of life, jumping from stone to stone, slipping on this rock, and falling into that pool, because their line was so long they could do nothing with it — a line that reached down forty years, sometimes. Now, if you would avoid these difficulties, *shorten your line!* Let it reach over one day only; for "sufficient unto the day is the evil thereof." To the man who is living weeks or years in advance of the present, God says, "Go back, go back to your duties. Work while the day lasts, and take no thought for the morrow. *I* am master down here."

WHAT trees are in summer, covered with leaves and blossoms, exhaling perfume, and filled with merry birds that sing out of their hidden choirs, are Conscience, Veneration, Fear even, when they are shined upon by Love; but, without love, any of these faculties is like that tree in winter, through which the wind whistles and the storm — gaunt, leafless, bloodless.

"BE ye kindly affectioned one towards another," does not refer to an occasional impulse, but to a reservoired state of feeling, out of which the various parts of life ought to flow. Christian graces should be like Croton water, which presses from the reservoir on every faucet in the city. Each one should be full and ready for use when needed, whereas they are too often like a pump run down and need a deal of working before they can supply our need.

LABORED sermons sometimes sweep over the mind as winds sweep over the sea, leaving it more troubled than before; when one little hymn, child-warbled, would be to the soul like Christ's "Peace, be still," to the waves of Galilee.

THERE is no class in society who can so ill afford to undermine the conscience of the community, or to set it loose from its moorings in the eternal sphere, as merchants, who live upon confidence and credit. Any thing which weakens or paralyzes this, is taking beams from the foundations of the merchant's own warehouse.

AN oak tree for two hundred years grows solitary. It is bitterly handled by frosts; it is wrestled with by ambitious winds, determined to give it a downfall. It holds fast and grows alone. "What avails all this sturdiness?" it saith to itself. "Why am I to stand here useless? My roots are anchored in rifts of rocks; no herds can lie down under my shadow; I am far above singing birds, that seldom come to rest among my leaves; I am set as a mark for storms, that bend and tear me; my fruit is serviceable for no appetite; it had been better for me to have been a mushroom, gathered in the morning for some poor man's table, than to be a hundred-year oak, good for nothing."

While it yet spoke, the axe was hewing at its base. It died in sadness, saying as it fell, "Weary ages for nothing have I lived."

The axe completed its work. By and by the trunk and root form the knees of a stately ship, bearing the country's flag around the world. Other parts form keel and ribs of merchantmen, and having defied the mountain storms, they now equally resist the thunder of the waves and the murky threat of scowling hurricanes. Other parts are laid into floors, or wrought into wainscoting, or carved for frames of noble pictures, or fashioned into chairs that embosom the weakness of old age. Thus the tree, in dying, came not to its end, but to its beginning of life. It voyaged the world. It grew to parts of temples and dwellings. It held upon its surface the soft tread of children and the tottering steps of patriarchs. It rocked in the cradle. It swayed the limbs of age by the chimney corner, and heard, secure within, the roar of those old, unwearied tempests that once surged about its mountain life. Thus, after its growth, its long uselessness, its cruel prostration, it became universally helpful, and did by its death what it could never have done by its life. For, so long as it was a tree, and belonged to itself, it was solitary and useless; but when it gave up its own life, and became related to others, then its true life began.

How solemn is that sentence of Christ, "And I, if I be lifted up from the earth, will draw all men unto me"! Not while he lived; not by his direct force, but only when pierced, broken, slain, buried, should his influence issue forth, and death should become the throne of his power. So will it be with us if we are Christ's. Paradoxes upon this truth lie all through the New Testament, and one may walk on them, like stepping stones, from side to side. Sorrow is joy. Death is life. Down is up. Weakness is strength. Loss is gain. Defeat is victory. The world's mightiest men, the very monarchs of its joy, were they who died deaths daily.

"I CAN forgive, but I cannot forget," is only another way of saying, "*I will not forgive.*" A forgiveness ought to be like a cancelled note, torn in two and burned up, so that it never can be shown against the man.

NEXT to victory, there is nothing so sweet as defeat, if only the right adversary overcomes you.

WHEN we are pierced with afflictions, the way is not to go to God and say, "Take away this thorn!" God says, "No. I put it there to bleed you where you are plethoric."

Suffering well borne is better than suffering removed. Suffering did not slip in, as theologians make so many things to have done, at the fall; but it is a part of God's original method. I know enough of gardening to understand that if I would have a tree grow upon its south side I must cut off the branches there. Then all its forces go to repairing the injury, and twenty buds shoot out where otherwise there would have been but one. When we reach the garden above, we shall find that out of those very wounds over which we sighed and groaned on earth, have sprung verdant branches, bearing precious fruit, a thousand fold.

SUFFERING, in this world, is both remedial and penal. When it is rightly received it is remedial. When it is resisted, it becomes penal to him who resists, and admonitory to the spectator.

Suffering is the jarring of the faculties of the mind one upon another, and it never will cease till they are all tuned to harmony. There are two ways of escaping from suffering; the one by rising above the causes of conflict, the other by sinking below them; for there is quiet in the soul whenever all its faculties are harmonized about any centre. The one is the religious method; the other is the vulgar, worldly method. The one is called Christian elevation; the other stoicism.

God's promises are the comfort of my life. Without them I could not stand for an hour in the whirl and eddy of things, in the sweep and surge of the nations; but I cannot tell *how* he will fulfil them, any more than I can tell from just what quarter the first flock of bluebirds will come in the spring. Yet I am sure that the spring will come upon the wings of ten thousand birds.

Let every man come to God in his own way. God made you on purpose, and me on purpose, and he does not say to you, "Repent, and feel as Deacon A feels," or, "Repent, and feel as your minister feels," but, "Come just as you are, with *your* mind, and heart, and education, and circumstances."

You are too apt to feel that your religious experience must be the same as others have; but where will you find analogies for this? Certainly not in nature. God's works do not come from his hand like coins from the mint. It seems as if it were a necessity that each one should be in some sort distinct from every other. No two leaves on the same tree are precisely alike; no two buds on one bush have the same unfolding, nor do they seek to have.

What if God should command the flowers to appear before him, and the sunflower should come bending low with shame because it was not a violet, and the violet should come striving to lift itself up to be like a sunflower, and the lily should seek to gain the bloom of the rose, and the rose the whiteness of the lily; and so, each one, disdaining itself, should seek to grow into the likeness of the other. God would say, "Stop, foolish flowers! I gave you your own forms, and hues, and odors, and I wish you to bring what you have received. O sunflower, come as a sunflower; and you, sweet violet, come as a violet; and let the rose bring the rose's bloom, and the lily the lily's whiteness." Perceiving their folly, and ceasing to long for what they had not, violet and rose, lily and geranium, mignonette and anemone, and all the floral train, would come, each in in its own loveliness, to send up its fragrance as incense, and all to wreathe themselves in a garland of beauty about the throne of God.

Now, God speaks to you as to the flowers, and

says, "Come with the form and nature that I gave you. If you are made a violet, come as a violet. If you are a rose, come as a rose. If you are a shrub, do not desire to be a tree. Let every thing abide in the nature which I gave it, and grow to the full excellence that is contained in that nature."

The popular impression is, that grace is designed to change men *from* nature. No. They are sinful simply because they have deviated from their true nature, or fallen short of it. Grace is given to bring out the fulness of every man's nature. Not the nature which schoolmen write about; but that nature which God thought of when he put forth man, and pronounced him a child of God, bearing his Father's likeness.

Men are not so much mistaken in desiring to advance themselves as in judging what will be an advance, and what the right method of it. An ambition which has conscience in it will always be a laborious and faithful engineer, and will build the road, and bridge the chasms between itself and eminent success by the most faithful and minute performances of duty. The liberty to go higher than we are is given only when we have fulfilled amply the duty of our present sphere. Thus men are to rise upon their performances, and not upon their discontent. And this is the secret and golden meaning of the command to be *content* in whatever sphere we are placed. It is not to be the content of indifference, of indolence, of unambitious stupidity, but the content of industrious fidelity. When men are building the foundations of vast structures, they must needs labor far below the surface, and in disagreeable conditions. But every course of stone which they lay raises them higher; and at length, when they reach the surfacc, they have laid such solid work under them that they need not fear now to carry up their walls, through towering stories, till they overlook the whole neighborhood. A man proves himself fit to go higher who shows that he is faithful where he is. A man that will not do well in his present place, because he longs to be higher, is fit neither to be where he is nor yet above it; he is already too high, and should be put lower.

MANY people use their refinements as a spider uses his web — to catch the weak upon, that they may be mercilessly devoured. Why not, rather, as the silkworm uses its web? It lives to spin it, and dies that it may yield it for others' benefit.

It is not wrong that men who have intellectual powers and tastes like ours should become agreeable to us; but that those who have them not should become to us disagreeable is wrong. Every man should use his intellect, not as those who study in their libraries, when all the world is asleep, use their lamps, for their own seeing only; but as light-houses use their lanterns, that those who are far off upon the deep may see the shining, and learn their way. God appoints our graces to be nurses to other men's weaknesses.

A RELIGIOUS life is not a thing which spends itself like a bright bubble on the river's surface. It is rather like the river itself, which widens continually, and is never so broad or so deep as at its mouth, where it rolls into the ocean of eternity.

MEN are afraid of slight outward acts which will injure them in the eyes of others, while they are heedless of the damnation which throbs in their souls in hatreds, and jealousies, and revenges.

They are more troubled by the outburst of a sinful disposition, than by the disposition itself. It is not the evil, but its reflex effect upon themselves, that they dread. It is the love of approbation, and not the conscience, that enacts the part of a moral sense, in this case. If a man covets, he steals. If a man has murderous hate, he murders. If a man broods dishonest thoughts, he is a knave. If a man harbors sharp and bitter jealousies, envies, hatreds, though he never express them by his tongue, or shape them by his hand, they are there. Society, to be sure, is less injured by their latent existence than it would be by their overt forms. But the man himself is as much injured by the cherished thoughts of evil, in his own soul, as by the open commission of it, and sometimes even more. For evil brought out ceases to disguise itself, and seems as hideous as it is. But evil that lurks and glances through the soul avoids analysis, and evades detection.

There are many good-seeming men who, if all their day's thoughts and feelings were to be suddenly developed into acts, visible to the eye, would run from themselves, as men in earthquakes run from the fiery gapings of the ground, and sulphurous cracks that open the way to the uncooled centre of perdition.

PRIDE slays thanksgiving, but a humble mind is the soil out of which thanks naturally grow. A proud man is seldom a grateful man, for he never thinks he gets as much as he deserves. When any mercy falls, he says, "Yes, but it ought to be more. It is only manna as large as a coriander seed, whereas it ought to be like a baker's loaf."

How base a pool God's mercies fall into, when they plash down into such a heart as that!

If one should give me a dish of sand, and tell me there were particles of iron in it, I might look for them with my eyes, and search for them with my clumsy fingers, and be unable to detect them; but let me take a magnet and sweep through it, and how would it draw to itself the almost invisible particles, by the mere power of attraction! The unthankful heart, like my finger in the sand, discovers no mercies; but let the thankful heart sweep through the day, and as the magnet finds the iron, so it will find in every hour some heavenly blessings; only the iron in God's sand is gold.

THERE are many Christians who, all their life long, carry their hope as a boy carries a bird's nest containing an unfledged bird that can scarcely peep, much less sing — a poor, fledgeless hope.

WE must not make the ideas of contentment and aspiration quarrel, for God made them fast friends.

A man may aspire, and yet be quite content until it is time to rise. A bird that sits patiently while it broods its eggs flies bravely afterwards, leading up its timid young. And both flying and resting are but parts of one contentment. The very fruit of the gospel is aspiration. It is to the human heart what spring is to the earth; making every root, and bud, and bough desire to be more.

REPENTANCE is neither base nor bitter. It is good rising up out of evil. It is the resurrection of your thoughts out of graves of lust. Repentance is the turning of the soul from the way of midnight to the point of the coming sun. Darkness drops from the face, and silver light dawns upon it. Do not live, day by day, trying to repent, but fearing the struggle and the suffering. Deferred repentance, in generous natures, is a greater pain than would be the sorrow of real repentance. Manly regret for wrong never weakens, but always strengthens the heart. As some plants of the bitterest root have the whitest and sweetest blossoms, so the bitterest wrong has the sweetest repentance, which, indeed, is only the soul blossoming back to its better nature.

CHRIST never seems to us so sweet and glorious, as when he orbs himself over the sea of our sinfulness and ingratitude.

NOT parties, but principles. Let us be of no party but God's party, and use all other agencies as we use railroad cars — travelling upon one train as far as it will take us in the right direction, and then leaving it for another.

WHEN we think of the labor required to rear the few that are in our households, — the weariness, the anxiety, the burden of life, — how wonderful seems God's work! for he carries heaven, and earth, and all realms in his bosom.

Many think that God takes no thought for any thing less than a star or a mountain, and is unmindful of the little things of life; but when I go abroad, the first thing which I see is the grass beneath my feet, and, nestling in that, flowers smaller yet, and, lower still, the mosses with their inconspicuous blooms, which beneath the microscope glow with beauty. And if God so cares for "the grass of the field, which to-day is, and to-morrow is cast into the oven," shall he not much more care for the minutest things of your life, "O ye of little faith"?

EVERY child walks into existence through the golden gate of love, else it would seem wonderful that the helpless thing should be born. Yet children are not playthings, as we too often seem to think they are — mere gifts of God to fill up the hours with cheer. They were surely meant to be a pleasure to us, but that is not the final end. Nor were they meant to be cares and burdens alone. To speak of them as if they were shackles and fetters upon our freedom; always in the way; "children, children, every where," is a shame and a sin. They are to be regarded as a part of our education. Men cannot be developed perfectly who have not been compelled to bring children up to manhood. You might as well say that a tree is a perfect tree without leaf or blossom, as to say that a man is a man who has gone through life without experiencing the influences that come from bending down, and giving one's self up to those who are helpless and little.

Children make men better citizens. When your own child comes in from the street, and has learned to swear from the boys congregated there, it is a very different thing to you from what it was when you heard the profanity of those boys as you passed them. Now it makes you feel that you are a stockholder in the public morality. Of what use would an engine be to a ship, if it were lying loose in the hull? It must be fastened to it with bolts and screws, before it can propel the vessel. Now, a childless man is like a loose engine. A man must be bolted and screwed to the community before he can work well for its advancement; and there are no such screws and bolts as children.

A GREAT deal of our heart life is cryptogamous — mosses and inconspicuous blooms hidden in the grass, thoughtlets, the *intents* of the heart. We are hardly aware of this life; but as God sees in winter all the flowers which are yet sleeping beneath the soil, so he sees all the hidden feelings of our hearts. He knows every root, and what will spring from it, and comprehends its intents, which are yet but germs, as well as its thoughts, which have already blossomed.

SOME people think black is the color of heaven, and that the more they can make their faces look like midnight, the more evidence they have of grace. But God, who made the sun and the flowers, never sent me to proclaim to you such a lie as that. We are told to "rejoice in the Lord always." What then? "And again I say, Rejoice." Thus, in a message in which there was time for but two things, both of them were joy. The test of your Christian character should be, that you are a joy-bearing agent to the world.

THE discipline of this world is to take a creature born in a physical condition, and to develop in him the higher life of the affections, until he can use the inward faculties, instead of the outward senses, to recognize truth. This is called faith; and, instead of faith's being a difficult thing, a man has to throw the dead wood of logic and of scepticism right across the current of his life to prevent him from exercising it.

Do not come to me, and tell me you are fit to join the church because you love to pray morning and night. Tell me what your praying has *done* for you; and then call your neighbors, and let me hear what they think it has done for you.

IF a thing reflects no light, it is black; if it reflects part of the rays, it is blue, or indigo, or red; but if it reflects them all, it is white. If we are like Christ, we shall seek, not to absorb, but to reflect the light which falls upon us from heaven upon others, and thus we shall become pure and spotless; for this is the meaning of the "white robes" which the saints wear in glory.

A BABE is a mother's anchor. She cannot swing far from her moorings. And yet a true mother never lives so little in the present as when by the side of the cradle. Her thoughts follow the imagined future of her child. That babe is the boldest of pilots, and guides her fearless thoughts down through scenes of coming years. The old ark never made such voyage as the cradle daily makes.

WITH every child we lose we see deeper into life, as with every added lens we pierce farther the sky.

GOD will accept your first attempt, not as a perfect work, but as a beginning. The beginning is the promise of the end. The seed always whispers "oak," though it is going into the ground, acorn. I am sure that the first little blades of wheat are just as pleasant to the farmer's eyes, as the whole field waving with grain.

WE grieve that our days are so inharmonious. Our hearts are continually going in and out, as it were, of eclipses. Yesterday jostles to-day, and to-morrow will carry them both away captive.

MAY God make us patient to live. Not that we should not have aspirations; but till the flying comes, let us brood contentedly upon our nests.

WHEN Allston died, he left many pictures which were mostly sketches, yet with here and there a part finished up with wonderful beauty. So I think Christians go to heaven with their virtues mostly in outline, only here and there a part completed. But "that which is in part shall be done away," and God shall finish the pictures in his own forms and colors.

EVERY use of the past which leaves you with the feeling of the past, is a wrong use. If you take the suffering and death of Christ in the old Jerusalem aright, they will lead you to the new Jerusalem, where he ever liveth to make intercession for us. Because the Bible came to us from the past, we are not to seek God backwards, as if Christ were living in his eighteen hundred years ago, and Jehovah, wrapped in the mantle of four thousand years, dwelt upon Sinai. God is the eternal *now*, and we are to look up and forward for the ever-living Saviour.

A CHRISTIAN man's life is laid in the loom of time to a pattern which he does not see, but God does; and his heart is a shuttle. On one side of the loom is sorrow, and on the other is joy; and the shuttle, struck alternately by each, flies back and forth, carrying the thread, which is white or black, as the pattern needs; and in the end, when God shall lift up the finished garment, and all its changing hues shall glance out, it will then appear that the deep and dark colors were as needful to beauty as the bright and high colors.

No man is perfect. The ideal man is the whole Christian brotherhood. That alone presents God's idea in the creation of man.

WHAT wonderful provision God has made for us, spreading out the Bible into types of nature!

What if every part of your house should begin

to repeat the truths which have been committed to its symbolism? The lowest stone would say, in silence of night, "Other foundation can no man lay." The corner stone would catch the word, "Christ is the corner stone." The door would add, "I am the door." The taper burning by your bedside would stream up a moment to tell you, "Christ is the light of the world." If you gaze upon your children, they reflect from their sweetly-sleeping faces the words of Christ, "Except ye become like little children." If, waking, you look towards your parents' couch, from that sacred place God calls himself your father and your mother. Disturbed by the crying of your children, who are affrighted in a dream, you rise to soothe them, and hear God saying, "So will I wipe away all tears from your eyes in heaven." Returning to your bed, you look from the window. Every star hails you, but, chiefest, "the bright and morning Star." By and by, flaming from the east, the flood of morning bathes your dwelling, and calls you forth to the cares of the day, and then you remember that God is the sun, and that heaven is bright with his presence. Drawn by hunger, you approach the table. The loaf whispers as you break it, "Broken for you," and the wheat of the loaf sighs, "Bruised and ground for you." The water that quenches your thirst says,

"I am the water of life." If you wash your hands, you can but remember the teachings of spiritual purity. If you wash your feet, that hath been done sacredly by Christ, as a memorial. The very roof of your dwelling hath its utterance, and bids you look for the day when God's house shall receive its top stone.

Go forth to your labor, and what thing can you see that hath not its message? The ground is full of sympathy. The flowers have been printed with teachings. The trees, that only seem to shake their leaves in sport, are framing divine sentences. The birds tell of heaven with their love-warblings in the green twilight. The sparrow is a preacher of truth. The hen clucks and broods her chickens, unconscious that to the end of the world she is part and parcel of a revelation of God to man. The sheep that bleat from the pastures, the hungry wolves that blink in the forest, the serpent that glides noiselessly in the grass, the raven that flies heavily across the field, the lily over which his shadow passes, the plough, the sickle, the wain, the barn, the flail, the threshing floor, all of them are consecrated priests, unrobed teachers, revelators that see no vision themselves, but that bring to us thoughts of truth, contentment, hope, and love. All are ministers of God. The whole earth doth praise him, and show forth his glory!

Dr. Kane, finding a flower under the Humboldt glacier, was more affected by it because it grew beneath the lip and cold bosom of the ice than he would have been by the most gorgeous garden bloom. So some single struggling grace, in the heart of one far removed from divine influences, may be dearer to God than a whole catalogue of virtues in the life of one more favored of Heaven.

---

* Let us interrupt the flow of the week, and rear up another Sabbath in the middle of it. And, as those who swim mighty streams do stop, panting, to rest upon some midway rock ere they plunge again into the tide, so let us rest here, lifted up above the tumult of earthly care, and gain strength, before we go down again into the dark ford, for the farther shore — the Sabbath.

If a bell were hung high in heaven which the angels swung whenever a man was lost, how incessantly would it toll in days of prosperity for men gone down, for honor lost, for integrity lost, and for manhood lost, beyond recall! But in times of dis-

* Addressed to the church at a Wednesday evening lecture.

aster the sounds would intermit, and the angels looking down would say, "He that findeth his life shall lose it, but he that loseth his life for my sake shall find it."

Do you ask me whether I would help a slave to gain his freedom? I answer, I would help him with heart, and hand, and voice. I would do for him what I shall wish I had done, when, having lost his dusky skin and blossomed into the light of eternity, he and I shall stand before our Master, who will say, "Inasmuch as ye did it unto him, slave as he was, ye did it unto me."

THERE is an ugly kind of forgiveness in this world — a kind of hedgehog forgiveness, shot out like quills. Men take one who has offended, and set him down before the blowpipe of their indignation, and scorch him, and burn his fault into him; and when they have kneaded him sufficiently with their fiery fists, then — they forgive him.

THE man who throws his plans into the current of divine Providence, will never want room to float his hull.

MEN often abstain from the grosser vices as too coarse and common for their appetites, while the vices which are frosted and ornamented are served up to them as delicacies.

IT is with the singing of a congregation as with the sighing of the wind in the forest, where the notes of the million rustling leaves, and the boughs striking upon each other, altogether make a harmony, no matter what be the individual discords.

LAWS and institutions are constantly tending to gravitate. Like clocks, they must be occasionally cleansed, and wound up, and set to true time.

MANY people are afraid to embrace religion, for fear they shall not succeed in maintaining it.

Does the spring say, "I will not come unless I can bring all fruits and sheaves under my wings?" No. She casts down loving glances in February, and in March she ventures near in mild days, but is beaten back and overthrown by storm and wind. Yet she returns, and finally yields the earth to April, far readier for life than she found it. The rains are still cold, but the grass is growing green, and the buds are swelling. In May the air is yet chilly, but it has the odor of flowers, and every day grows warmer till the delicious June, when all is bloom and softness, and even the storms have nourishment in them. Then come the glowing July and the fervid August, followed by the glorious autumn of harvest and victory!

And shall nature do so much, while we dare not attempt to overcome the coldness and deadness of our hearts, and to fill them with the summer of love?

WHEN flowers are full of heaven-descended dews, they always hang their heads; but men hold theirs the higher the more they receive, getting proud as they get full.

THE aster has not wasted spring and summer because it has not blossomed. It has been all the time preparing for what is to follow, and in autumn it is the glory of the field, and only the frost lays it low. So there are many people who must live forty or fifty years, and have the crude sap of their natural dispositions changed and sweetened before the blossoming time can come; but their life has not been wasted.

When people undertake to restrain themselves without knowing how, they are often worse off than if they had let themselves alone; just as a stream, when you throw a little dam across it, bubbles and plunges all the more.

Worldly joy is like the songs which peasants sing, full of melodies and sweet airs. Christian joy has its sweet airs too; but they are augmented to harmonies, so that he who has it goes to heaven, not to the voice of a single flute, but to that of a whole band of instruments, discoursing wondrous music.

God puts the excess of hope in one man in order that it may be a medicine to the man who is despondent.

If some cynical people had been by when God was making the human mind, as he took up Faith, they would have said, "Put in that," and as he took up Conscience, "Put in that," and Fear, "Put in that;" but as he took up Mirthfulness, they would have touched his arm and said, "Don't put that in!" Fortunately, such people were not the counsellors of God. Mirthfulness is in the mind, and you cannot get it out. It is the blessed spirit that God has set in the mind to dust it, to enliven its dark places, and to drive asceticism, like a foul fiend, out at the back door. It is just as good, in its place, as Conscience or Veneration. Praying can no more be made a substitute for smiling, than smiling can for praying.

Do not be troubled because you have not great virtues. God made a million spears of grass where he made one tree. The earth is fringed and carpeted, not with forests, but with grasses. Only have enough of little virtues and common fidelities, and you need not mourn because you are neither a hero nor a saint.

I USED to think the Lord's Prayer was a short prayer; but, as I live longer, and see more of life, I begin to believe there is no such thing as getting through it. If a man, in praying that prayer, were to be stopped by every word until he had thoroughly prayed it, it would take him a lifetime. "Our Father" — there would be a wall a hundred feet high in just those two words to most men. If they might say, "Our Tyrant," or "Our Monarch," or even "Our Creator," they could get along with it;

but "Our *Father*" — why, a man is almost a saint who can pray that.

You read, "Thy will be done," and you say to yourself, "O, I can pray that;" and all the time your mind goes round and round in immense circuits and far-off distances; but God is continually bringing the circuits nearer to you, till he says, "How is it about your temper and your pride? How is it about your business and your daily life?"

This is a revolutionary petition. It would make many a man's shop and store tumble to the ground to utter it. Who can stand at the end of the avenue along which all his pleasant thoughts and wishes are blossoming like flowers, and send these terrible words, "Thy will be done," crashing down through it? I think it is the most fearful prayer to pray in the world.

Every well-doer on the face of the earth is my blood relation through Jesus Christ. I feel his heart beating right up to my ribs, and mine beating back to his. All the good passed away and transfigured into glory are mine. My own mother is not more really, though more tenderly, mine, than is the mother of St. Chrysostom or St. Augustine; and

I belong to every man at whose soul God's angel has knocked, so that he has received the divine life.

WHEN a man's pride is thoroughly subdued, it is like the sides of Mount Etna. It was terrible while the eruption lasted and the lava flowed; but when that is past, and the lava is turned into soil, it grows vineyards and olive trees up to the very top.

MEN have different spheres. It is for some to evolve great moral truths, as the heavens evolve stars, to guide the sailor on the sea and the traveller on the desert; and it is for some, like the sailor and the traveller, simply to be guided.

YOU are in a hurry to see the world in its latter-day glory; and well you may be, for you have but a little time. But God is not in a hurry. There is no such thing as *time* with God. The world is his seed-bed. He has planted deep and multitudinously, and many things there are which have not yet come up. Some things are just sprouted, and some have blossomed; and yet, because the sheeted prairie of life is not covered with the flowers of love, men say, "It will never come. The world will be burned up first."

The world is preparing day by day for the millennium, but you do not see it. Every season forms itself a year in advance. The coming summer lays out her work during the autumn, and buds and roots are forespoken. Ten million roots are pumping in the streets; do you hear them? Ten million buds are forming in the axils of the leaves; do you hear the sound of the saw or the hammer? All next summer is at work in the world, but it is unseen by us, and so "the kingdom of God cometh not with observation."

If any man is rich and powerful, he comes under that law of God by which the higher branches must take the burnings of the sun, and shade those that are lower; by which the tall trees must protect the weak plants beneath them.

Patriotism, in our day, is made to be an argument for all public wrong, and all private meanness. For the sake of country a man is told to yield every thing that makes the land honorable. For the sake of country a man must submit to every ignominy that will lead to the ruin of the state through disgrace of the citizen. There never was a man so unpatriotic as Christ was. Old Jerusalem ought to have been every thing to him. The laws and institutions of his country ought to have been more to him than all the men in his country. They were not, and the Jews hated him; but the common people, like the ocean waters, moved in tides towards his heavenly attraction wherever he went.

OUR children that lie in the cradle are ours, and bear in them those lines which shall yet make them to appear, the boy like the father, and the daughter like the mother; and we are God's, growing up, we trust, into the lineaments which shall make us like unto him. "It doth not yet appear what we shall be."

WHENEVER education and refinement grow away from the common people, they are growing towards selfishness, which is the monster evil of the world.

Men who walk on tiptoe all through life, holding up their skirts for fear they shall touch their fellows, who are delicate and refined in feeling, and who ring all the bells of taste high up in their own belfry, where no one else can hear them, — these dainty fools are the greatest sinners of all, for they use their higher faculties to serve the devil with.

MAN is God's creation. Every thing else is the nursery and nurse of man.

I NEVER knew my mother. She died when I was three years old that she might be an angel to me all my life. But one day, in after years, turning over a pile of old letters in my father's study, I found a package of her letters to him, beginning with her first acquaintance with him, and coming down into her married life; and as I read those pages, at last I knew my mother.

What these letters were to her life, that are the four Gospels to the life of Christ. But I remember that there was one letter in which she first spoke freely and frankly of her love. That, to me, is the Gospel of John. It is God's love-letter to the world.

A MAN'S purpose of life should be like a river, which was born of a thousand little rills in the mountains; and when at last it has reached its manhood in the plain, though, if you watch it, you shall see little eddies that seem as if they had changed their minds, and were going back again to the mountains, yet all its mighty current flows, changeless, to the sea. If you build a dam across it, in a few hours it will go over it with a voice of victory. If tides check it at its mouth, it is only that when they ebb it can sweep on again to the ocean. So goes the Amazon or the Orinoco across a continent — never losing its way or changing its direction for the thousand streams that fall into it on the right hand and on the left, but only using them to increase its force, and bearing them onward in its resistless channel.

A NOBLE man compares and estimates himself by an idea which is higher than himself, and a mean man by one which is lower than himself. The one produces aspiration; the other, ambition. Ambition is the way in which a vulgar man aspires.

FROM the beginning, I educated myself to speak along the line, and in the current of my moral convictions; and though, in later days, it has carried me through places where there were some batterings and bruisings, yet I have been supremely grateful that I was led to adopt this course. I would rather speak the truth to ten men than blandishments and lying to a million. Try it, ye who think there is nothing in it; try what it is to speak with God behind you — to speak so as to be only the arrow in the bow which the Almighty draws.

A Christian had better go to the theatre than to go home whining because he *can't* go. If it is worth while to do any thing for Christ, it is worth while to do it with your head up, and with your whole heart.

It takes only one good, thorough frost to cut all the flowers out of the garden — no thanks to the second; so one thoroughly-detected dissimulation in love, and honey is vinegar, and love is gall.

O, let the soul alone. Let it go to God as best it may. It is entangled enough. It is hard enough for it to rise above the distractions which environ it. Let a man teach the rain how to fall, the clouds how to shape themselves and move their airy rounds, the seasons how to cherish and garner the universal abundance, but let him not teach a soul to pray, on whom the Holy Ghost doth brood!

In autumnal mornings mists settle over the Connecticut Valley, and lie cold and damp upon the meadows and the hill sides, and it is not till the sun rises and shines down warm upon them that they begin to move; and then there are swayings, and wreathings, and openings, till at length the spirit which has tormented the valley can stay no longer, but rises and disappears in the air. So is it when the Sun of Righteousness shines upon the troubles which brood over our souls. Shining but a little, they only fluctuate; but if the sun will shine long, they lift themselves and vanish in the unclouded heaven.

Selfishness is that detestable vice which no one will forgive in others, and no one is without in himself.

Like a plant in the tropics which all the year round is bearing flowers, and ripening seeds, and letting them fly, so the heart is always shaking off memories and dropping associations. And as the wind which serves to prostrate a plant is only a sower coming forth to sow its seeds, planting some of them in rock crevices, some by river courses, some among mossy stones, some under warm hedges, and some in garden and open field, — so it is with our experiences of life, that sway and bow us, either with joy or sorrow. They plant every thing about us with heart seeds. Thus a house becomes sacred. Every room has a thousand memories. Every door and window is clustered with associations. And when, after long years, we go back to the house of our infancy, faces look out upon us, and an invisible multitude stand in gate and portal to welcome us, and we hear airy voices speaking again the old words of our childhood. Every man has a silent and solitary literature written by his heart upon the tables of stone in nature; and next to God's finger, a man's heart writes the most memorable things.

WHEN the people pass wise and needful laws, but leave them without public sentiment, it is as if a child were born into an exhausted receiver instead of a cradle.

IF there is one word that is universally significant of love, peace, refinement, social amenity, friendship, pure society, joy, it is the table. Such power has the heart to clothe the most unseemly things with its own vines and fragrant flowers, that we have not only forgotten that eating is an animal act, but we have come to associate every thing that is sweet and beautiful with it. We no longer think of appetite, but of love. It is not food, but society that we have. We cover the merest animal necessities with such sympathies, tastes, conversations, and gayeties, that the table, the symbol of appetite, has cleared itself from all grossness, and stands in the language of the world as the centre of social joy. A feast becomes sacred to hospitality. A festival is a religious observance.

A MAN living at a hotel is like a grape vine in a flower pot — movable, carried around from place to place, docked at the root and short at the top. Nowhere can a man get real root-room, and spread out his branches till they touch the morning and the evening, but in his own house.

As flowers never put on their best clothes for Sunday, but wear their spotless raiment and exhale their odor every day, so let your Christian life, free from stain, ever give forth the fragrance of the love of God.

WHEN the absent are spoken of, some will speak gold of them, some silver, some iron, some lead, and some always speak dirt, for they have a natural attraction towards what is evil, and think it shows penetration in them. As a cat watching for mice does not look up though an elephant goes by, so they are so busy mousing for defects, that they let great excellences pass them unnoticed. I will not say it is not *Christian* to make beads of others' faults, and tell them over every day; I say it is *infernal.* If you want to know how the devil feels, you *do know* if you are such an one.

THE more important an animal is to be, the lower is its start. Man, the noblest of all, is born lowest. The next thing below a babe is nothing, and the next thing above a man is an angel.

LOOKED at without educated associations, there is no difference between a man in bed and a man in a coffin. And yet, such is the power of the heart to redeem the animal life, that there is nothing more exquisitely refined, and pure, and beautiful, than the chamber of the house. The couch! From the day that the bride sanctifies it to the day when the aged mother is borne from it, it stands clothed with loveliness and dignity. Cursed be the tongue that dares speak evil of the household bed! By its side oscillates the cradle. Not far from it is the crib. In this sacred precinct, the mother's chamber, lies the heart of the family. Here the child learns its prayer. Hither, night by night, angels troop. It is the Holy of Holies.

Wherever I find truth, I will appropriate it, for it is an estray from God's word, and belongs to me and to all. Eminent masters, parties, and sects claim truths as theirs, because they have most fully expounded them; but men never make truths; they only recognize the value of this currency of God. They find truths as men sometimes find bills, in the street, and only recognize the value of that which other parties have drawn.

Very few men acquire wealth in such a manner as to receive pleasure from it. Just as long as there is the enthusiasm of the chase they enjoy it; but when they begin to look around, and think of settling down, they find that that part by which joy enters is dead in them. They have spent their lives in heaping up colossal piles of treasure, which stand, at the end, like the pyramids in the desert sands, holding only the dust of kings.

God has put the veil of secrecy before the soul for its preservation; and to thrust it rudely aside, without reason, would be suicidal. Neither here, nor, as I think, hereafter, will all our thoughts and feelings lie open to the world.

The common school stands on the threshold of society, and throws each generation back to the one starting-point, and says to it, "Now come up because of what is in you." Who can estimate the power of an institution that is continually evening one end of life, but leaving the other to shoot up as plants do from the common soil?

What would the nightingale care if the toad despised his singing? He would sing on, and leave the cold toad to his dank shadows. And what care I for the sneers of men who grovel upon earth? I will still sing on into the ear and bosom of God.

Men do not avail themselves of the riches of God's grace. They love to nurse their cares, and seem as uneasy without some fret, as an old friar would be without his hair girdle. They are commanded to cast their cares upon the Lord; but, even when they attempt it, they do not fail to catch them up again, and think it meritorious to walk burdened. They take God's ticket to heaven, and then put their baggage on their shoulders, and tramp, tramp, the whole way there afoot.

THE stream of life forks; and religion is apt to run in one channel, and business in another.

IT is one of the severest tests of friendship to tell your friend of his faults. If you are angry with a man, or hate him, it is not hard to go to him and stab him with words; but so to love a man that you cannot bear to see the stain of sin upon him, and to speak painful truth through loving words,—that *is* friendship. But few have such friends. Our enemies usually teach us what we are, at the point of the sword.

I THINK I heard a conversation in the leaves this morning, as I came to church. The buds that had lain all winter in their wrappings, as under roofs and blankets, were beginning to say to each other, "Is it not March? Is it not time for us to unfold ourselves, and expand our leaves in fragrance to the air?"

But one tiny bud answered, "I can never unfold to the sun and the air these dear little leaves, that have lain so long in my bosom. I could not bear such publicity. I must keep their fragrance still." And the sun and the wind laughed; for they knew that when they should shine and blow upon the bud, and fill up and swell those tiny leaves, it would open from the necessity of its nature, and that when they were swimming in a bath of solar light, they would give out their odor unconsciously to every breeze.

So many a heart says, "I could not bear to have my sweet buds of feeling exposed, through profession of Christianity, to the gaze of the world. I will keep them safely hid in my bosom, and be a Christian in secret." But when the winds of heaven blow upon them, and the sun of God's love shines, they will become vocal, and must needs give themselves expression.

THERE are many here to-day who know not yet what fruit they shall bear; may the gracious Husbandman take care of all these tender shoots and buds of spring. And there are those who are in the summer of their growth, and who spread abroad their leaves and expand their blossoms; may God grant them the gracious rains of heaven, that they may be nourished, and sustained, and brought to all perfection. And there are those who stand in autumn, with clustering fruits and glowing colors; may He minister to them all those influences which are needful for the autumn of their experience, and bring them gloriously to the end of the harvest. And there are those who are in life's winter, and whose leaves have fallen, and through whose unclothed boughs the sunlight shines; O thou who art the God of winter as well as of summer, be very near to them till thou dost take them to the land where no winter comes!

AMID our imperfect utterances, let us comfort ourselves with the thought of that realm where thought shall speak without the need of a tongue, and feeling shall speak, and the whole life shall be an anthem of praise.

OUR most exalted feelings are not meant to be the common food of daily life. Contentment is more satisfying than exhilaration; and contentment means simply the sum of small and quiet pleasures.

We ought not to seek too high joys. We may be bright without transfiguration. The even flow of constant cheerfulness strengthens; while great excitements, driving us with fierce speed, both rack the ship and end often in explosions. If we were just ready to break out of the body with delight, I know not but we should disdain many things important to be done. Low measures of feeling are better than ecstasies, for ordinary life. God sends his rains in gentle drops, else flowers would be beaten to pieces.

SINK the Bible to the bottom of the ocean, and man's obligations to God would be unchanged. He would have the same path to tread, only his lamp and his guide would be gone; he would have the same voyage to make, only his compass and chart would be overboard.

LOVE is ownership. We own whom we love. The universe is God's because he loves.

---

* CHRISTIAN brethren, in heaven you are known by the name of Christ. On earth, for convenience'

* Invitation to the communion service.

sake, you are known by the name of Presbyterians, Episcopalians, Methodists, Congregationalists, and the like. Let me speak the language of heaven, and call you, simply, Christians. Whoever of you has known the name of Christ, and feels Christ's life beating within him, is invited to remain, and sit with us at the table of the Lord.

---

*My friends, my heart is large to-day. I am like a tree upon which rains have fallen till every leaf is covered with drops of dew; and no wind goes through the boughs but I hear the pattering of some thought of joy and gratitude. I love you all more than ever before. You are crystalline to me. Your faces are radiant; and I look through your eyes as through windows into heaven. I behold in each of you an imprisoned angel, that is yet to burst forth, and to love and shine in the better sphere.

The whole earth is like a caldron, boiling and seething with human passions. Man is at war with man, and every where are rage and animosity. When, from God's fatherhood, shall come the truth

* At communion, when one hundred were added to the church.

of our brotherhood? Lord Jesus, what hast thou done since thou wentest away? Hast thou forgotten thine errand hither? Art thou not weary of this globe, which swings about thy throne on its bitter path with anthems of pain and woe? Hasten the time when the whole world, en-choired by love, shall go its golden way, singing thy praise and its joy!

THE real man is one who always finds excuses for others, but never excuses himself.

MEN'S convictions of sin differ with their characters. One man says, "In such a sermon, a lion-like conviction sprang out upon me, and seized my soul in its grasp, and had nearly torn it asunder." And another says, "The twilight of God's love fell upon me; but when the eclipse was over, the sun shone out again, and I was happy." Terror, or only sadness, anguish, grief, and love, are all alike really conviction.

WE have known men, upon whose grounds were old, magnificent trees of centuries' growth, lifted up into the air with vast breadth, and full of twilight at midday, who cut down all these mighty monarchs, and cleared the ground bare; and then, when the desolation was completed, and the fierce summer gazed full into their faces with its fire, they bethought themselves of shade, and forthwith set out a generation of thin, shadowless sticks, and pined and waited till they should stretch out their boughs with protection, and darken the ground with grateful shadow. Such folly is theirs who refuse the tree of life, the shadow of the Almighty, and sit, instead, under feeble trees of their own planting, whose tops will never be broad enough to shield them, and whose boughs will never discourse to them the music of the air.

The mountains lift their crests so high, that weary clouds, which have no rest in the sky, love to come to them, and, wrapping about their tops, distil their moisture upon them. Thus mountains hold commerce with God's invisible ocean, and, like good men, draw supplies from the unseen. So, in times of drought below, the rocks are always wet, the mountain moss is always green, the seams and crevices are always dripping, and veins are throbbing a full pulse, while all the summer down in the plains faints for want of moisture. In some virgin gorge, unwedded by the sun, cold rills bubble up and issue forth upon their errand. Could one who would build his house below but meet these springs in the mountains, and lay his artificial channels to their very sources, he would not know when drought came, for they never grow dry so long as clouds brood the mountain tops. Day and night they gush and fall with liquid plash, an unheard music, except when thirsty birds, to whose song the rivulet has been a bass, stoop to drink at their crystal edges.

Artificial cisterns dry up and crack for dryness; but this mountain fountain comes, night and day, with cool abundance. While others with weary strokes force up from deep wells a penurious supply of turbid water, he that has joined himself to the mountain spring has its voice continually in his dwelling, night and day, summer and winter, without work or stroke of laboring pump, clear, sweet, and cheerful, running of its own accord; and singing at its work, more musical than any lute, and bringing in its song suggestions of its home — the dark recess, the rock which was its father, the cloud which was its mother, and the teeming heaven bright and broad above both rock and cloud.

With such a spring, — near, accessible, urging itself upon eye and ear, — how great would be his folly who should abandon it, and fill his attic with a leaden cistern, which forever leaked when full, and was dry when it did not leak! Yet this is what we have done. We have forsaken God, "the fountain of living waters, and hewed us out cisterns, broken cisterns, that can hold no water."

HAPPINESS is not the end of life; character is. This world is not a platform where you will hear Thalberg-piano-playing. It is a piano manufactory, where are dust, and shavings, and boards, and saws, and files, and rasps, and sand-papers. The perfect instrument and the music will be hereafter.

GOD asks no man whether he will accept life. That is not the choice. You *must* take it. The only choice is *how*.

THE other day, in walking down the street, a little beggar boy, — or one who might have begged, so ragged was he, — having discovered that I loved flowers, came and put into my hand a faded little sprig which he had somewhere found. I did not look directly at the scrawny, withered branch, but beheld it through the medium of the boy's heart, seeing what he would have given, not what he gave; and so looking, the shrivelled stem was laden with blossoms of beauty and odor. And if I, who am cold, and selfish, and ignorant, receive so graciously the offering of a poor child, with what tender joy must our heavenly Father receive the sincere tributes of his creatures when he looks through the medium of his infinite love and compassion!

Christ does not say, "Take the noblest things of life, and bring them perfect to me, and I will receive them." He says, "Take the lowest and most disagreeable thing; and if you bring it cheerfully, for my sake, it shall be to me a flower of remembrance, and I will press it in the book of life, and keep it forever."

Go, then, search for flowers to bring to Christ; and if you cannot find even road-side or pasture weeds,—if there are but nettles and briers, and you are willing for his sake to thrust your hand into the thorn bush, and bring a branch from thence, he will take it lovingly, and cherish it evermore.

LET me fall into the hands of God, and not of man; yet even there, such is the heart's weakness that we must often cry out, "O, remember that we are but dust." Let God deal with me in the street, in the door-yard,—yea, let him come into the house, and deal with me in the parlor,—but let him not come into my chamber, and deal with me in the cradle. Then he is a terrible God; and I tremble, and shrink away from his presence.

There is an anger that is damnable; it is the anger of selfishness. There is an anger that is majestic as the frown of Jehovah's brow; it is the anger of truth and love.

If a man meets with injustice, it is not required that he shall not be roused to meet it; but if he is angry after he has had time to think upon it, that is sinful. The flame is not wrong, but the coals are.

There are men who imagine they should do well enough if they could throw the Bible overboard, and the ministers after it, and sink the whole church in the sea. It is as if a man with a shattered limb should think to better himself by thrusting the doctors and their instruments out of doors. They did not break his leg, but only propose to set it. Under the hand of the poorest of them, the limb will be better than if the shattered bone were left to heal unsplintered.

It is supposed that if a man is a Christian, he must perform certain professional duties which are no more to be expected of a man who is not a Christian than a lawyer's duties are expected of a mechanic. Now, all the great duties of a Christian life are no more incumbent upon Christians than upon other men; for men are bound to be and do right on the religious scale of rectitude, not because they are *Christians*, but because they are *men*. Religious obligations took hold of us when we were born. They waited for us as the air did. They have their sources back of volition, back of consciousness, just as attraction has. Though a man declares himself an atheist, it in no way alters his obligations. Right and wrong do not spring from the nature of the church. Obligation lies deeper than that. The church is a mere organization to help a man fulfil his duties; it is not the source from whence those duties sprang. If there is any thing in your business, or your character, which you would feel that you ought to change if you were a Christian, you ought to change it now. It is as much the worldling's duty to love God and to obey his laws, as it is the Christian's. An unpraising heart! You do not need to have been baptized, to be damned, if you have that.

As we do not keep tinder in every box in the house, so we do not keep the sense of anger in

14

every faculty. When one comes against the door of some faculties with an injury, we look over the railing and say, —

"I'll forgive you for that, for you did not get in."

But by and by, when the faculty where we are sensitive is entered, then we grind our teeth and say, —

"I could have forgiven him for any thing but that!"

We must not arrogate to ourselves a spirit of forgiveness, until we have been touched to the quick where we are sensitive, and borne it meekly; and meekness is not mere white-facedness, a mere contemplative virtue; it is maintaining peace and patience in the midst of pelting provocations.

MOZART and Raphael! As long as the winds make the air give forth sounds, and the sun paints the earth with colors, so long shall the world not let these names die.

SEE to it that each hour's feelings, and thoughts, and actions are pure and true; then will your life be such. The mightiest maze of magnificent harmonies that ever a Beethoven gave to the world, is but single notes, and all its complicated and interlacing strains are resolvable into individualities. The wide pasture is but separate spears of grass; the sheeted bloom of the prairies but isolated flowers.

THE vertical power of Christianity with Christians, will measure its horizontal power in the world.

WE rejoice in God since he has taught us that every thing which is true in us, is but a faint expression of what is in him. And thus all our joys become to us the echo of higher joys, and our very life is as a dream of that nobler life, to which we shall awaken when we die.

WE are apt to believe in Providence so long as we have our own way; but if things go awry, then we think, if there is a God, he is in heaven, and not on earth.

The cricket in the spring builds his little house in the meadow, and chirps for joy, because all is going so well with him. But when he hears the sound of the plough a few furrows off, and the thunder of the oxen's tread, then the skies begin to look dark, and his heart fails him. The plough comes craunching along, and turns his dwelling bottom side up, and as he goes rolling over and over without a home, he says, —

"O, the foundations of the world are destroyed, and every thing is going to ruin!"

But the husbandman who walks behind the plough, singing and whistling as he goes, does he think the foundations of the world are breaking up? Why, he does not so much as know there was any house or cricket there. He thinks of the harvest which is to follow the track of the plough; and the cricket, too, if he will but wait, will find a thousand blades of grass where there was but one before.

We are like the crickets. If any thing happens to overthrow *our* plans, we think all is going to ruin.

THERE is always somebody to believe in any one who is uppermost.

THERE is no greater crime than to stand between a man and his development; to take any law or institution and put it around him like a collar, and fasten it there, so that as he grows and enlarges, he presses against it till he suffocates and dies.

We ought not to judge men by their absolute excellence, but by the distance which they have travelled from the point at which they started. There are some men whom God has so royally endowed that they are like a bird sitting on the topmost branch of the forest, and if God says to it, "Mount up," it has nothing to do but to spring into the air, singing as it goes towards heaven. But others are like a bird upon the ground, that has to disentangle itself from the bushes, and then to work its way among the darkling boughs, before it can soar. The one may have done better by his outward wings, but the better inward wings of purpose and endeavor beat far stronger in the other, and bring him quite as near to God; for God dwells beneath the shade, as much as above the forest.

We are all building a soul-house for eternity; yet with what different architecture and what various care!

What if a man should see his neighbor getting workmen and building materials together, and should say to him, "What are you building?" and he should answer, "I don't exactly know. I am waiting to see what will come of it." And so walls rush up, and room is added to room, while the man looks idly on, and all the bystanders exclaim, "What a fool he is!" Yet this is the way many men are building their characters for eternity, adding room to room, without plan or aim, and thoughtlessly waiting to see what the effect will be. Such builders will never dwell in "the house of God, not made with hands, eternal in the heavens."

Many men build as cathedrals were built, the part nearest the ground finished; but that part which soars towards heaven, the turrets and the spires, forever incomplete.

A kitchen, a cellar, a bar, and a bedroom; these are the whole of some men, the only apartments in their soul-house.

Many men are mere warehouses full of merchandise — the head, the heart, are stuffed with goods. Like those houses in the lower streets of the city which were once family dwellings, but are now used for commercial purposes, there are apartments in their souls which were once tenanted by taste, and love, and joy, and worship, but they are all deserted now, and the rooms are filled with earthy and material things.

He who selfishly hoards his joys, thinking thus to increase them, is like a man who looks at his granary, and says, "Not only will I protect my grain from mice and birds, but neither the ground nor the mill shall have it." And so, in the spring, he walks around his little pit of corn, and exclaims, "How wasteful are my neighbors, throwing away whole handfuls of grain!" But autumn comes; and, while he has only his few poor bushels, their fields are yellow with an abundant harvest. "There is that scattereth and yet increaseth."

CHRISTIANS! it is your duty not only to be good, but to shine; and, of all the lights which you kindle on the face, Joy will reach farthest out to sea, where troubled mariners are seeking the shore. Even in your deepest griefs, rejoice in God. As waves phosphoresce, let joys flash from the swing of the sorrows of your souls.

IN human governments, justice is central, and love incidental. In the divine government, love is the central element, and justice only incidental. God wishes to exhaust all means of kindness before his hand takes hold on justice. When the waves of penalty begin to come in in fearful tides, then he banks up against them. His goodness is the levee between justice and the sinful soul.

Does love implead with God for us, as it does in us for those we hold dear? Does he look wistfully forth to see when such and such an one shall leave earth and come to him — as parents, waiting for vacation, look every hour along the road to watch for their children?

If we are Christ's, every passing day brings us nearer to him, and he is gathering up our treasures in heaven. When any thing falls overboard from a ship upon the sea, it goes astern; but when any thing drops into the ocean of life, it is taken up, and carried forward to wait for us. And when that which we call death, comes, it is Christ's summons. He wants us to come to him. To some of us it has been a long voyage. A few more watches, and it will be ended, and there will rise the cry of "Land, ho!" more rapturous than ever greeted an earthly shore. And then may we hear, sweeter than the songs of myriad angels, the voice of One who has longed for us, and for whom we have been home-sick, — the voice of our Saviour, — saying to us, "Welcome, ye blessed of my Father. Enter ye into the joy of your Lord."

God sends Experience to paint men's portraits. Does some longing youth look at the settled face of a Washington, whose lineaments have been transmitted to us by the artist's skill, and strive to wear as noble a mien? That look,—the winds of the Alleghanies, the trials of the Jersey winter, the sufferings at Cambridge, the conflicts with Congress, wrought it out; and he who would gain it must pass through as stern a school.

I SOMETIMES go musing along the street to see how few people there are whose faces look as though any joy had come down and sung in their souls. I can see lines of thought, and of care, and of fear,—money lines, shrewd, grasping lines,—but how few happy lines! The rarest feeling that ever lights the human face is the contentment of a loving soul. Sit for an hour on the steps of the Exchange in Wall Street, and you will behold a drama which is better than a thousand theatres, for all the actors are real.

THE light falls on the skin of the Anglo-Saxon, and the rays are reflected, and he is white. The same light falls on the skin of the negro, and the rays are absorbed, and he is black; and morals and religion, on a national scale, are modified by a reflecting or non-reflecting cuticle. If the African race had been as handsome as the Circassian, there would not to-day be a single slave among them. Beauty is omnipotent. Pards and tigers are fabled to have drawn the cars of the wreathed and graceful Bacchanals, in ancient song; and to-day, among unsanctified men, truth and justice love beauty better than they love themselves.

Whether the Africans are an inferior race or not, it is evident that our destiny in some respects is bound up with them, and the study of their interests is the study of our salvation. When a ship casts its passengers overboard in a storm, there may be sick and helpless ones among them who could not for a moment compete with the robust swimmers; but the feeblest of them, by attaching themselves to the swimmers, may embarrass them, and make them go down. So this African race, in the Omnipotent hand, may be the instrument for our destruction, if we are to be destroyed. They may cling to our feet, and entangle us in their final miseries.

Truths are first clouds, then rain, then harvests and food. The philosophy of one century is the common sense of the next. Men are called fools, in one age, for not knowing what they were called fools for averring in the age before. We should so live and labor in our time that what came to us as seed may go to the next generation as blossom, and that what came to us as blossom may go to them as fruit. This is what we mean by progress.

DEATH is the dropping of the flower that the fruit may swell.

IF men whose sympathy is strong for their fellows have been to churches where they have heard the preaching of dry doctrines, — if the tree of life has been to them a girdled tree, leafless, and without birds in its boughs, — they are very apt to ignore doctrine, and to go to the opposite extreme, and say, "It's well enough to sing hymns, and there's no harm in prayers, perhaps; but the best hymns and prayers are to do good." It is very true that to love justice and to show mercy is more than all sacrifice of hymns and prayers; yet, as the world goes, I have noticed that most men decry the one, only for the sake of covering their neglect of the other.

I AM suspicious of that church whose members are one in their beliefs and opinions. When a tree is dead, it will lie any way; alive, it will have its own growth. When men's deadness is in the church, and their life elsewhere, all will be alike. They can be cut and polished any way. When they are alive, they are like a tropical forest — some shooting up, like the mahogany tree ; some spreading, like the vine ; some darkling, like the shrub ; some lying, herb-like, on the ground ; but all obeying their own laws of growth, — a common law of growth variously expressed in each, — and so contributing to the richness and beauty of the wood.

It makes no difference what you call men — prince, peer, or slave. *Man* is that name of power which rises above them all, and gives to every one the right to be that which God meant he should be. No law, nor custom, nor opinion, nor prejudice has the right to say to one man, "You may grow," and to another, "You may not grow," or, "You may grow in ten directions, and not in twenty;" or to the strong, "You may grow stronger," or to the weak, "You may never become strong." Launched upon the ocean of life, like an innumerable fleet, each man may spread what sails God has given him, whether he be pinnace, sloop, brig, bark, ship, or man-of-war; and no commodore or admiral may signal what voyage he shall make or what canvas he shall carry.

God has given to men the great truths of liberty and equality, which are like mothers' breasts, carrying food for ages. Let us not fear that in our land they shall be overthrown or destroyed. Though we may go through dark times, — rocking times, when we are seasick, — yet the day shall come when there shall be no more oppression, but when, all over the world, there shall be a common people, sitting in a commonwealth, having a common Bible, a common God, and common peace and joy in a common brotherhood!

The world is so fruitful that we can hardly even blunder without bringing forth some good. We can take up no scheme, however wild and impracticable, but it will strike off some flower or fruit from the tree of knowledge.

It often happens that the coming of Christ to his disciples, for their relief, is that which frightens them most, because they do not know the extent of God's wardrobe; for I think that as a king might never wear the same garment but once, in order to show his riches and magnificence, so God comes to us in all exigencies, but never twice alike. He sometimes puts on the garments of trouble; and, when we are calling upon him as though he were yet in heaven, he is walking by our side; and that from which we are praying God to deliver us is often but God himself. Thus it is with us as with children who are terrified by their dreams in the night, and scream for their parents, until, fully waking, behold they are in their parents' arms!

QUESTIONS of future society are too vast to be determined by the present. Society, like life, grows from a principle divinely implanted, and all we can do is to stimulate and tend it. God never gives us the light which our children need; he gives it to them.

THERE are multitudes of men like the summer vines, which never grow even ligneous, but stretch out a thousand little hands to grasp the stronger shrubs; and if they cannot reach them, they lie dishevelled in the grass, hoof-trodden, and beaten of every storm.

It does not tarnish bright gifts to hold them in restraint lest their heedless liberty should injure others. Men who would cheerfully forego lawful pleasures which injure the weak, often feel that it is reversing the law of growth, and the divine method, to shape the pattern of our life, not upon the large pattern of our own powers, but upon the meagre pattern of the ignorant, the prejudiced, and the vulgar. And yet, every man should learn better from the nursery, in which God teaches men more deep theology than all books contain, of the nobleness of strength nourishing weakness, of knowledge careful of ignorance, and of experience waiting upon childhood, and, by serving it with all self-renunciation, gaining honor and greatness. As yet, the world will not understand that he governs whom love makes serviceable. The strong are few, the weak are many; and God appoints the strong to serve the weak, saying, "We, then, that are strong ought to bear the infirmities of the weak, and not to please ourselves. Let every one of us please his neighbor for his good to edification. For even Christ pleased not himself; but, as it is written, The reproaches of them that reproach thee fell on me."

THERE are some who stand on a narrow strip of land between two dead seas, and drink their waters alternately. The past is filled with bitter regrets, and ghosts which will not be laid, but walk still to haunt them; and the future is filled with shadowy shapes, which beckon them forward to new suffering. There is a purgatory, and it is this: it is the point where good, despaired of, touches evils remembered.

PIETY may be called the act of right-growing. It is moving towards true attainment that constitutes it.

SUPPOSE a man should sail, all the boiling and blazing day, round and round an old Dutch ship in the harbor, and the next day you should see him, like a magnified fly, creeping up and down the masts, and spars, and examining the rigging, and you should ask him what he was doing, and he should answer, "I have heard that this ship is a dull sailer, and I want to look at it and see." Could he ever find out in this way? No. Let him weigh anchor and spread the canvas, and take the wind and bear away, if he would know how she sails.

So, if a Christian would learn his true state, let him not row round and round the hull of his self-consciousness, and creep up and down the masts and spars of his feelings and affections; but let him spread the sails of resolution, and bear away on the ocean of duty. Then he shall know whether he be a dull or a fast sailer.

SOME regard religion as a sort of divine aura, which descends upon a man and encircles him, as silvery mists enwreathe autumnal mountain tops. There is a sense in which this is true. No one would become a Christian without the direct aid of the Holy Spirit, any more than a bud would become a blossom without the influence of the sun; but yet, personal religion is the result of personal choice.

A STATE in which the citizen is the pabulum of the state, will soon have nothing left to feed on.

THE church was built to disturb the peace of man; but often it does not perform its duty, for fear of disturbing the peace of the church. What kind of artillery practice would that be which declined to fire for fear of kicking over the gun carriages, or waking up the sentinels asleep at their posts?

A CHURCH may have a creed that shall be like Jacob's ladder, uniting earth and heaven, and angels of exposition may run nimbly up and down upon it before the congregation; and yet, if there is no love in that church, unlike the patriarch, it will never wake from its sleep, or lift its head from the pile of stones on which it lies.

MANY men are swamped in the doctrines of election and predestination, but this is supreme impertinence. They are truths which belong to God, and if you are troubled by them, it is because you are meddling with what does not belong to you. You only need to understand that all God's agencies are to assist you in gaining your salvation, if you will but use them rightly. To doubt this is as if men in a boat, pulling against the tide, and, with all their efforts, going backwards every hour, should by and by find the current turning, and see the wind springing up with it and filling the sails, and hear the man at the helm exclaim, "Row away, boys! Wind and tide are in your favor," and they should all say, "What shall we do with the oars? Do not the wind and the tide take away our free agency?"

WHEN Christ came, it was not necessary for him to teach that man was miserable, any more than it would be to demonstrate the presence of disease in a hospital of fevered, palsied patients; for, in addition to the woes of the individual, the world was a tangled web of misery. Each year travailed in pain, and passed the legacy to the next, and the centuries rolled on with this weight of woe. And still the world looks desolate. The ages seem only to burden it as they march over, while God's promises hang above it like stars, distant and cold. Yet we believe in him, and, like the prophets of old, we stand and cry, "How long, O Lord, how long!"

CHARACTER, like porcelain ware, must be painted before it is glazed. There can be no change after it is burned in.

WE are not sent into life as a butterfly is sent into summer, gorgeously hovering over the flowers, as if the interior spirits of the rainbow had come down to greet these kisses of the season upon the ground; but to labor for the world's advancement, and to mould our characters into God's likeness, and so, through toil and achievement, to gain happiness. I would rather break stones upon the road, if it were not for the disgrace of being in a chain gang, than to be one of those contemptible joy-mongers, who are so rich and so empty that they are continually going about to find something to make them *happy*.

One should go to sleep at night as homesick passengers do, saying, "Perhaps in the morning we shall see the shore." To us who are Christians, it is not a solemn, but a delightful thought, that perhaps nothing but the opaque, bodily eye prevents us from beholding the gate which is open just before us, and nothing but the dull ear prevents us from hearing the ringing of those bells of joy which welcome us to the heavenly land. That we are so near death, is too good to be believed.

God does not refuse to make himself known to man. He only will not do it by the symbolism of matter. He comes to us at once by the most natural course. We are in a transient state; our bodies are accidental, and God comes to us by that which is higher and truer — the intuitions of the soul.

Men's graces must get the better of their faults as a farmer's crops do of the weeds — by growth. When the corn is low, the farmer uses the plough to root up the weeds; but when it is high, and shakes its palm-like leaves in the wind, he says, "Let the corn take care of them," for the dense shadow of growing corn is as fatal to weeds as the edge of the sickle.

* In looking upon a congregation like this, it is natural to think of you as you appear in the world; here a merchant, there a teacher; here a mechanic, there an artist; here a shipmaster, there a banker. But to-night I seem to behold you in your higher relations, and you stand to me like living portraits on the background of eternity. I behold the lines of God in your faces. No longer are you to me men of the street, or of the house, but creatures of heaven; and, like a flock of birds in autumn sitting upon the bough, with wings half-lifted, waiting for the migratory hour, I see you just ready to take flight for the eternal land!

There is dew in one flower and not in another, because one opens its cup and takes it in, while the other closes itself, and the drops run off. God rains his goodness and mercy as wide-spread as the dew, and if we lack them, it is because we will not open our hearts to receive them.

The great men of earth are the shadowy men, who, having lived and died, now live again and forever through their undying thoughts. Thus living,

* At the close of a Sabbath evening sermon.

though their footfalls are heard no more, their voices are louder than the thunder, and unceasing as the flow of tides or air.

Moses was not half living when he was alive. His real life has been since he died. The prophets seemed almost useless in their time. They did little for themselves or for the church of that day; but when you look at the life they have lived since, you shall find they have been God's pilots, guiding the church through all perils. From their black bosoms they sent forth the blast of his lightning and the roar of his thunder; and to-day, if the church needs rebuke and denunciation, it is they who must hurl it. I could have killed old Jeremiah, if I could have got at his ribs; but I should like to see the archer that could hit him now. Martin Luther was mighty when he lived; but the shadowy Luther is mightier than a regiment of fleshly Luthers. When he was on earth, he in some sense asked the pope leave to be, and the emperor and the elector leave to be; he asked the stream and the wheat to give him sustenance for a day; but now that his body is dead, — now that that rubbish is out of the way, — he asks no leave of pope, or elector, or emperor, but is the monarch of thought, and the noblest defender of the faith to the end of time.

I KNOW it is more agreeable to walk upon carpets than to lie upon dungeon floors; I know it is pleasant to have all the comforts and luxuries of civilization; but he who cares only for these things is worth no more than a butterfly, contented and thoughtless upon a morning flower; and who ever thought of rearing a tombstone to a last summer's butterfly?

WHAT we call wisdom is the result, not the residuum, of all the wisdom of past ages. Our best institutions are like young trees growing upon the roots of the old trunks that have crumbled away.

Do you ever reflect that your powers of accomplishment are direct mercies from Heaven? God does a more wonderful thing when he holds all your faculties in such nice adjustment and perfect play that you win success, than he would have done if he had wrought the fruit of that success himself by a miracle.

To the infidel, Nature's voices are but a Babel din. Trees rustle, and brooks babble, and winds blow; but there is no meaning in their sound. To the Christian, all speak of God; and if it were not for the dimness of the natural eye, he might see his hosts of angels at their ministry. The tree stretches out its arm, laden with fruit, like the arm of God. The morning sprinkles him with dew, as with holy water; and he is sung to sleep, at evening, with songs like the lullaby of earthly parents to their children.

As flowers carry dewdrops, trembling on the edges of the petals, and ready to fall at the first waft of wind or brush of bird, so the heart should carry its beaded words of thanksgiving; and at the first breath of heavenly favor, let down the shower, perfumed with the heart's gratitude.

It is a solemn thing to be married; to have to preach to a congregation from your own loins; to have God put the hand of ordination on you in the birth of your children, and say to you, "Now art thou a priest unto those whom I have given thee."

If ever the stream of life should flow like crystal water over shining stones, it should be the stream of daily life in the family. If God has taught us all truth in teaching us to love, then he has given us an interpretation of our whole duty in our own households. We thank him that we are not born as the partridge of the wood, or the ostrich of the desert, to be scattered every whither; but that we are grouped together and brooded by love, and reared day by day in that first of churches, the family.

Of all earthly music, that which reaches the farthest into heaven is the beating of a loving heart.

In our land, men have classified themselves. We have aristocrats, but God made them; and there never will be a time when mightiness of soul shall not overshadow littleness of soul. It was designed that some should be high, some intermediate, and some low, as trees are some forty, some a hundred, and some, the giant pines, (how solitary their tops must be!) three hundred feet in height. But, however high their tops may reach, their roots rest in the same soil; as men, though they can grow and tower aloft as much as they please, still stand on a common level.

Do the best you can where you are; and, when that is accomplished, God will open a door for you, and a voice will call, "Come up hither into a higher sphere."

SIMPLY weed a man, so that he shall produce nothing evil, but never plant him, so that he shall produce something good, and what is he worth? If this be cultivation, the Desert of Sahara is the most perfectly cultivated spot on the globe.

ONE of the best prayers ever offered is that which Christ himself hallowed, and set apart for our observation — "God be merciful to me, a sinner!" There is no title, no "forever and ever, Amen," to it. It is only the heart broken out of the man.

ALL the sobriety which religion needs or requires, is that which real earnestness produces. Tears and shadows are not needful to sobriety. Smiles and cheerfulness are as much its elements. When men say, Be sober, they usually mean, Be stupid; but when the Bible says, Be sober, it means, Rouse up, and let fly the earnestness and vivacity of life. The old, scriptural sobriety was effectual *doing;* the later, ascetic sobriety is effectual *dulness.*

ONE of our great troubles, as ministers, is to keep people from wishing to be awfully converted. There are those who will not come into God's kingdom unless they can come as Dante went into paradise — by going through hell. They wish to walk over the burning marl, and to snuff the sulphureous air.

If a man has done wrong, his own thoughts should turn him to reparation; but if they do not, the first intimation from the injured friend should suffice. But if he will come to no terms until the matter has passed through the court, and the execution is in the hands of the officer, and then, at length, in the final extremity, yields, his yielding is the basest compliance of fear, and not the impulse of honor or conscience. And even more, men should be ashamed of needing deep convictions of sin before they repent before God. He must be a mean and a very wicked man who will not submit to God till he has been dealt with by such terrors. Magnanimous repentance never waits for the spur of remorse before it bounds towards the injured one, with confession and reconciliation.

I MARVEL how a woman, with her need of love, with her sensitive, yearning, clasping nature, can look into the face of the Lord Jesus, and not put her arms about his neck, and tell him, with gushing love, that she commits herself, body and soul, into his sacred keeping!

* This concert, I perceive by the notice, is to be "partly sacred and partly instrumental;" that is to say, one part is to be just as sacred as the other; for all good music is sacred, if it is heard sacredly, and all poor music is execrably unsacred.

The Bible Society is sending its shiploads of Bibles all over the world — to Greenland and the Morea, to Arabia and Egypt; but it dares not send them to our own people. The colporteur who should leave a Bible in a slave's cabin would go to heaven from the lowest limb of the first tree. It was hell, among the ancients, that was guarded by a hundred-headed dog; in this country, it is heaven that has the Cerberus.

Asceticism is not dead yet. A man may be poor in spirit without being poor in his garments. Because a man is a Christian he is not called to forswear the treasures of refinement. Consecrated using, and not despising and throwing away, is God's law for riches and beauty, and all earthly good. All secular good belongs to the Christian more than to any other man. In God's wish, he is

* Notice of a concert.

not only the heir of God hereafter, but it is declared that he shall now inherit the *earth.* A Christian who every day carries home his gifts to Christ may be heaped with treasure, and with all things that are beautiful in the world. The world only waits till Christians can bear it without self-indulgence, before it pours all its bright possessions into their lap. It is enough that Christ was born in a manger; his children are not always to tabernacle there. Christ is not to be the pauper of the universe forever. He is to be the King of glory.

THERE are some people who forever add a "*But then*" to every positive having, and so always make a drain or sluiceway by which the heavenly stream of God's favors escapes from them.

THE church has been so fearful of amusements that the devil has had the care of them. The chaplet of flowers has been snatched from the brow of Christ, and given to Mammon.

MANY people think that *doctrine* should be the staple of preaching, — that on a rainy day, or when the minister is not quite well, he can preach *morality*, — but that when he is strong and vigorous, and knows what he is about, he should preach doctrine. This doctrinal preaching may be food for one tenth of the congregation; but the nine tenths will be driven by it, through disgust, into moralities. It creates two distinct parties — the spiritualists, who are always looking Godward, and crying, "Thither, thither!" and the moralists, who look manward, and cry, "Hither, hither!" The one party lives in the *then*, the other party in the *now*. Both are right, — minister and people, — and both are wrong. Doctrines and moralities must be united.

Many ministers forge doctrines as they would forge ploughs. One Sunday it is election; and they heat it red hot, and beat and hammer it upon the anvil, and then put it away, cold iron, upon the shelf. The next Sunday it is decrees; and they beat and hammer that, and lay it also aside. The next Sunday it is the perseverance of the saints; and the next, the origin of evil, or some equally incomprehensible thing, for the farther a subject is from the range of human faculties the better it seems to be to make a doctrine of; and so they go on through the year, with occasional exceptions, and the next year they take them down and cast them over again. They do not use them. They only fashion them. They rub them up, they polish them, and then lay them again on the shelf — disputing meanwhile which pattern is best. There are various schools; and each school has its own pattern, and berates the others, without ever doing as inventors do at agricultural fairs — taking their ploughs out into the field with them, to see which can do the best work.

Now, I believe in doctrines, with my explanations, as much as they; but I must *use* them. My duty is to forge a plough, and then to give it a handle, and then to fasten a team to it strong as eternity, and to put it into the soil, and to rip through the sod down to the subsoil, and to roust out all the vermin and the nibbling mice, and turn up the yellow dirt to the sun.

No doctrine is good for any thing that does not leave behind it an ethical furrow ready for the planting of seeds which shall spring up and bear abundant harvests.

There are many of us whose children are in heaven, who have been borne from us through quick life to lie in angels' bosoms; and, though they were not wrested from us without pangs, and though the places which they filled in our hearts are as wells of tears, yet we would not have them back, and we are glad to-day for our sakes and for their own. And some we are piloting, but must soon leave them alone upon the tossing sea. God grant that then, without shipwreck, they may safely reach the haven where we have gone.

WHEN a church is faithless to its duties, the real church is outside its walls, in the community.

IN plan, include the whole; in execution, take life day by day. Men do not know how to reconcile the oppugnant directions that we should live for the future, and yet should find our life in fidelities to the present; but the last is only the method of the first. True aiming, in life, is like true aiming in marksmanship. We always look at the fore-sight of a rifle through the hind-sight.

THERE are many Christians who like, about once in twelve months, to have a good revival in their hearts. They think that, like the year, they can make up for freezing and snowing all winter by a period of intense heat in the summer. The remedy for such is not to chill the revivals, but to shorten the intervals between them, and to endeavor to make their life equatorial and tropical all the year round.

No one cries when children, long absent from their parents, go home. Vacation morning is a jubilee. But death is the Christian's vacation morning. School is out. It is time to go home. It is surprising that one should wish life here, who may have life in heaven. And when friends have gone out from us joyously, I think we should go with them to the grave, not singing mournful psalms, but scattering flowers. Christians are wont to walk in black, and sprinkle the ground with tears, at the very time when they should walk in white, and illumine the way by smiles and radiant hope. The disciples found angels at the grave of Him they loved; and we should always find them too, but that our eyes are too full of tears for seeing.

THE stars do not come to tell us that it is night, but to lay beams of light through it, and give the eye a path to walk in. It needed the mission of Christ to lift the darkness which brooded over the world, not to proclaim it; and therefore it was said, "To them which sat in the region and shadow of death light is sprung up." When men grope through the New Testament, and come forth with denials of man's wickedness, from the supposed lack of peremptory assertions, my reply to them would be, "Go, search all medical books; find me an argument to prove that there are fevers, or dropsies, or plagues. Search all military works, and find me the passages which laboriously seek to prove that men have been slain. Search through all optical works, and bring me the passage which declares that there is an eye, and that there is such an act as seeing." If there were as little common sense among men in every-day life as there is in their treatment of the Bible, the whole earth must needs become a lunatic asylum, to hold all who should be sent there.

NEVER forget what a man has said to you when he was angry. If he has charged you with any thing, you had better look it up. Anger is a bow that will shoot sometimes where another feeling will not.

THERE is many a Christian who has higher views of God in his closet, or on the sea, or when travelling through lonely woods, than he ever has in the sanctuary — outstartings, so to speak, of God before him, which reveal Him more plainly than any thing he ever found when he was seeking for Him.

SUFFERING is a part of the divine idea. All our faculties stand in a double constitution, and are just as really susceptible of pain as of pleasure. We were created so that every nerve was provided with this twofold nature, and both of them are divine. The world is filled full of dangerous things, — things which can bruise, and cut, and poison, — and no angel stands near them to say, "Come not here." There is not a step we can take but death is there. Pain is continually on the larboard or starboard side, and life consists in steering between dangers on the one hand or the other. Where there is so much sorrow, there is only one way. It is to think that suffering is a part of happiness. One who does this takes all trials, and heaps them up, and says, "They are no longer to me what they were before. They are not opaque; they are luminous."

A MAN in a state of hot-brain nervousness is burning up. He is like a candle in a hot candle-stick, which burns off at one end and melts down at the other.

It is a sad thing to look at some of the receiving hulks at the navy yard — to think that that was the ship which once went so fearlessly across the ocean! It has come back to be anchored in some quiet bay, and so roll this way and that with the tide. Yet this is what many men set before them as the end of life — that they may reach some haven, where they will be able to cast out an anchor at the bow and an anchor at the stern, and never move again; but rock lazily, without a sail, without a voyage, waiting simply for decay to take apart their timbers.

I have seen men who, I thought, ought to have a whole conversion for each one of their faculties. Their natures were so unmitigatedly wicked, that it cost more for them to be decent than it would for other men to be saints.

Public sentiment is like a battery, which protects the city that is behind it, but sweeps with destruction all the plain that is before it. It powerfully restrains men from doing wrong; but when they have done wrong, it sets itself as powerfully against them. The height of Dover Cliffs would prevent a man from jumping into the sea; but once amid the thunder of the waves, and what chance would there be for him to climb the steep?

MANY people regard the Bible as an old ruin. They think there may be some chambers in it which might be made habitable, if it were worth the while; but they take it as a young heir takes his estate, who says, "I shall build me a modern house to live in, but I'll keep the old castle as a ruin;" and so they have some scientific or literary house to live in, and look upon the Bible only as a romantic relic of the past.

A MAN must not only desire to be right — he must *be* right. You may say, "I wish to send this ball so as to kill the lion crouching yonder, ready to spring upon me. My wishes are all right, and I hope Providence will direct the ball." Providence won't. You must do it; and if you do not, you are a dead man.

MEN are greatly relieved when they have at length rid themselves of belief in some unwelcome doctrine — as if facts could be destroyed as easily as opinions.

God sees that you are naked and poor, and comes to you with a royal wardrobe and all supplies. Suppose you succeed in proving that there is no food or raiment; you are still poor and naked. What would you think, if there were to be an insurrection in a hospital, and sick man should conspire with sick man, and on a certain day they should rise up and reject the doctors and nurses! There they would be — sickness and disease within, and all the help without! Yet what is a hospital compared to this fever-ridden world, which goes swinging in pain and anguish through the centuries, where men say, "We have got rid of the atonement, and we are rid of the Bible"? Yes, and you have rid yourselves of salvation.

As, though the sky is not steadfastly clear, but often is covered with clouds, yet through the folds there shine at intervals the everlasting stars, so through the darkness of our hearts there steals at times the celestial glory, and we rejoice that there is a heaven above the world.

You know how the heart is subject to freshets; you know how the mother, who, always loving her child, yet, seeing in it some new wile of affection, will catch it up and cover it with kisses, and break forth in a rapture of loving. Such a kind of heart-glow fell from the Saviour upon that young man who said to him, "Good Master, what good thing shall I do that I may inherit eternal life?" It is said, "Then Jesus, beholding him, loved him."

SOME men spend their lives in picking off dead leaves from the tree of their being. They think they are growing better because they now and then take out their will, like a pruning knife, to cut off this and that bough. They imagine they are self-denying because they dust themselves over with unpleasant sulphur; but, all the while, they never go to the root, where the worm of selfishness is working.

THERE are many trials in life which do not seem to come from unwisdom or folly. They are silver arrows shot from the bow of God, and fixed inextricably in the quivering heart. They are to be borne. They were not meant, like snow on water, to melt as soon as they strike. But the moment an ill can be patiently borne, it is disarmed of its poison, though not of its pain.

THE thought of the future punishment for the wicked, which the Bible reveals, is enough to make an earthquake of terror in every man's soul. I do not accept the doctrine of eternal punishment because I delight in it. I would cast in doubts, if I could, till I had filled hell up to the brim. I would destroy all faith in it; but that would do me no good; I could not destroy the thing. Nor does it help me to take the word "everlasting," and put it into a rack like an inquisitor, until I make it shriek out some other meaning; I cannot alter the stern fact.

The exposition of future punishment in God's word is not to be regarded as a threat, but as a merciful declaration. If, in the ocean of life, over which we are bound to eternity, there are these rocks and shoals, it is no cruelty to chart them down; it is an eminent and prominent mercy.

THERE are no buds which can open without the sun, but there is a great difference in the time it takes them to unfold. Some have their outer petals so closely wrapped and glued together, that there must be many days of warm shining before they will begin to expand; and others there are which make haste to get out of the ground; and almost as soon as they are buds, they are blossoms. So is it with human hearts. Some are so cold and impervious that it seems as though God's Spirit never could reach them; and others there are which open to its first influences.

Some people have no perspective in their conscience. Their moral convictions are the same on all subjects. They are like a reader who speaks every word with equal emphasis.

Every thought and feeling is a painting stroke, in the darkness, of our likeness that is to be; and our whole life is but a chamber, which we are frescoing with colors that do not appear while being laid on wet, but which will shine forth afterwards, when finished and dry.

If there are any here this morning who are bewildered, and are wandering up and down in the forest of their own thoughts, sitting down to rest, and then rising again to renew their fruitless search for the path that leads out to light and joy, may the Shepherd of the lost go after them, and bring them back, if need be, in his own bosom. And if there are any who are in the garden, and, knowing not the Lord, are calling, "Tell me where they have laid him," may he speak to them by their names, that they may cry, "My Lord and my God!"

THERE is no day born but comes like a stroke of music into the world, and sings itself all the way through. There is no event that is discordant. All times and passages are full of melody, if we would but hear it. And as, in tumultuous floods and rushing falls of water, every drop is as obedient to the laws of nature as if it lay in the bosom of the tranquil lake, so all things in earth and in hell, in their wildest excesses as well as in their calmest flows, are obedient to God; and his providence is in them stately and serene, going on to its own ends and manifestations.

IT is winter now. The earth is frost-bound, and incrusted with ice and snow; but soon the sun will come wheeling from the tropics, and the voice of Spring will call, and the violets and daisies shall hear it, as well as the pines in Oregon, and every where there shall be life, and growth, and beauty.

So it is with man. His winter has been long and dark; but the sun of God's love shall shine, and the crusts of tyranny and the frosts of oppression shall melt away beneath its rays, and the humblest as well as the loftiest creature shall yet stand in the light and liberty of the sons of God.

LIKE gardens with high stone walls, very rich and pleasant to those who get in, but very unlovely and forbidding to those who are without, so are men of taste and cultivation, who spend their whole lives to themselves with knowledges and refinements most needful to common men, and employ all their pride to build themselves around inaccessible.

As, when our infant children are garnered in our bosoms, we do not bless them according to their capacity of asking, but according to the wealth of affection that is in our hearts for them, so does God, lifting us up and looking in our faces, bless us, not so much by what we need to receive, as by what he hath to give. Clouds never send down to ask the grass and plants below how much they need; they rain for the relief of their own full bosoms.

HEAVEN will be inherited by every man who has heaven in his soul. "The kingdom of God is within you."

THERE are hundreds of churches which are nothing but mutual insurance companies, seeking to take care of themselves and of each other, and to see that religion is protected. Religion protected! It was given us for *our* protection, and we are not to carry it unused and shielded from blows, but to put it on like armor, and to go down with it into the battle. When Paul said, "Quit ye like men," he was not thinking of those Christians who are rocked in the cradle of a conservative church, by the slippered foot of a soft-speaking minister, to all delicate ditties; but of a stalwart soldier, with his face as bronzed as his helmet, and ready for the fray.

It is not a man's part merely to keep his armor bright; to hang around the edge of the fight, and, whenever he sees it bulging out towards him, to retreat to a hill, and, if any dust has fallen upon his armor, to set to work at once to brush it off. It is a man's business to go down to the battle, and to use his sword when he gets there. Man was not meant to be an armor-keeper; but there are men who go all their lives scrubbing up their armor — keeping their hope bright and their faith bright, but never using them. Miserable, scouring Christians!

WHAT if the leaves were to fall a-weeping, and say, "It will be so painful for us to be pulled from our stalks, when autumn comes"? Foolish fear! Summer goes, and autumn succeeds. The glory of death is upon the leaves; and the gentlest breeze that blows takes them softly and silently from the bough, and they float slowly down, like fiery sparks, upon the moss.

It is hard to die when the time is not ripe. When it is, it will be easy. We need not die while we are living.

OUR business, as ministers, is not to make men a something else than men, called Christians; it is to take Christianity as a formative influence, by which to make men. They are re-created, it is true; but it is not out of manhood, but into manhood. Grace is meant to carry men back to nature, whose true laws and intents are only the moulds of God's thoughts. The idea of the Bible is not to make neat, snug, nice, dapper little Christians, that go tripping along the ways of life. There is no warrant in the Bible for any thing which is not manly, and robust, and large. Cautiousness and timidity, a narrow path and a timid policy, are not Christian traits.

---

* As bells answer bells, and strike with sweet collision in the air, so may heart answer heart, and joy answer joy, upon this wedding day, when those who are affianced to God are openly united to him in holy communion.

I HAVE seen men whose reverence for religion was so morbid that they could hardly lift up their eyes to heaven, but who made it up by the way they looked *down* on their fellow-men — men who yielded to no master here, who were touched by no name of friend or brother; but the moment the name of God was pronounced, they collapsed.

WHY should you carry troubles and sorrows unhealed? There is no bodily wound for which some herb doth not grow, and heavenly plants are more medicinal. Bind up your hearts in them, and they shall give you not only healing, but leave with you the perfume of the blessed gardens where they grew. Thus it may be that sorrows shall turn to riches; for

* At communion.

heart troubles, in God's husbandry, are not wounds, but the putting in of the spade before the planting of seeds.

MEN come to think that the guilt of sins committed in concert is distributed; and that if there be a thousand men banded and handed together in wickedness, each shall have but the one thousandth part of guilt. If a firm succeeds, the gain is distributed to each partner. But if it fails, each one may be held for the whole loss. Whoever commits a sin will bear the sin, whether alone or with a thousand. Whoever commits, or connives at a public sin, will bear the blame, as if he alone did it. Public guilt always has private indorsement, and each man is liable for the whole note.

No matter how good the walls and the materials are, if the foundations are not strong, the building will not stand. By and by, in some upper room, a crack will appear, and men will say, "There is the crack, but the cause is in the foundation." So, if in youth you lay the foundations of your character wrongly, the penalty will be sure to follow. The crack may be far down in old age, but somewhere it will certainly appear.

That which is called "public sentiment" is often nothing but a rod held over the head of approbativeness.

It is right to have an expansive benevolence, — to take into our regard the world and the race, — but where foreign charity is but a defence against home kindness, it is a base, sentimental sham. Thousands will cry over compressed feet in China who are quite unaffected by souls compressed in America. That religion should compel mothers, in India, to cast their babes to the Ganges, shocks every sensibility of some men's souls, who can see no occasion for grief that commerce snatches from the dusky mother in America her babes, and casts them forth to slavery — a worse monster than was ever bred in the slime of the Ganges or the mud of the Nile.

A Christian nation, jealous of its laws, but careless of its people, — conservative of its institutions, but contemptuous of the weak and poor whom those institutions oppress, — are baptized infidels. Christ never died for laws nor for governments, but for *men;* and they who crush men to build up nations may expect God to meet them with the blast of his lightning and the terror of his thunder. The masses against the classes, the world over, — I am willing to go to judgment upon that.

In the Bible, the word *doctrine* means simply *teaching*, *instruction.* It was a moral direction, a simple maxim, or a familiar practical truth. It certainly was not that thing which theologians have made doctrine to be — a mere philosophical abstraction. The doctrines which the schools teach are no more like those of the Bible than the carved beams of Solomon's temple were like God's cedar trees on Mount Lebanon. But men cut and hew till they have shaped their own fancies out of God's timber, and then they get upon them like judgment-day thrones, and call all the world to answer at their feet for heresies against their idols. There are few heresies in the world more real than the very idea of an abstract doctrine presented as God's truth. That way of thinking which men call metaphysics, seems not to be employed above. It is only a method of weakness down below. It is a preparation dissected and arranged for our microscope, who have not eyes strong enough to see things just as God made them, and just as he keeps them.

If a fireplace have a good chimney, the smoke will escape through the flue, and the room will have the benefit of the warmth and the ruddy light. So there are people who will be kind and good-natured to all about them, if you give them some single person on whom they may vent their impatience and peevishness. Otherwise they will fill the whole room with smoke. Social circles need chimneys as much as do houses.

THERE is nothing in this world so fiendish as the conduct of a mean man when he has the power to revenge himself upon a noble one in adversity. It takes a *man* to make a devil; and the fittest man for such a purpose is a snarling, waspish, red-hot, fiery creditor.

A LAW is valuable, not because it is law, but because there is right in it; and because of this rightness it is like a vessel carrying perfume — like the alabaster enclosure of a lamp. A principle is better than a rule; yet we are not to despise rules, for they are leading strings intended to bring us along the path of life to principles. A rule is like a mould. You pour in the wax; and when it is pressed, it comes out, and the mould is left behind. The end of a rule is to bring the man out from the rule. Rules are like sepals around a rose bud — good to keep the bud through its first stages; but when it opens, and comes to the perfect flower, then they fall off, and are useless. The highest type of character is that which is made up of feelings so luminous that the man takes a more elevated path than he could ever do if he were bound down to rules and precedents.

A MAN'S strength, in this life, is often greater from some single word, remembered and cherished, than in arms or armor. Looking over the dead on a field of battle, it was easy to see why that young man, and he a recruit, fought so valiantly. Hidden under his vest was a sweet face, done up in gold; and so, through love's heroism, he fought with double strokes, and danger mounting higher, till he found honor in death. So, if you carry the talisman of Christ in your heart, it will give you strength and courage in every conflict, and, at death, open to you the gates of glory.

LOVING is like music. Some instruments can go up two octaves, some four, and some all the way from black thunder to sharp lightning. As some of them are susceptible only of melody, so some hearts can sing but one song of love, while others will run in a full choral harmony.

* In commercial crises, manhood is at a greater discount than funds are. Suppose a man had said to me, last spring, "If there comes a pinch in your affairs, draw on me for ten thousand dollars,"— the man said so last spring, but I should not dare to draw on him this fall. I should say, "Times have changed; he would not abide by it." But God's promises are "from everlasting to everlasting," and he always stands up to them. There never was a run on heaven which was not promptly met. No creature in all the world, or in lying, audacious hell, shall ever say that he drew a draft upon heaven, and that God dishonored it.

How wonderful that Christ should love us! We know how to love our children, because they are better than we; we know how to love our friends, because they are no worse than we; but how Christ can stoop from out the circle of blessed spirits to love us, who are begrimed with sin, and bestormed with temptation, and wrestling with the lowest parts of humanity,—that is past our finding out. He has loved us from the foundation of the world; and because heaven was too far away for us to see, he came down to earth to do the things which he has

* From a sermon on the financial crisis, October, 1857.

always been doing profusely above. Christ's life on earth was not an official mission; it was a development of his everlasting state; a dip to bring within our horizon those characteristics and attributes which otherwise we could not comprehend; — God's pilgrimage on earth as a shepherd, in search of his wolf-imperilled fold. And when I look into his life, I say to myself, "As tender as this, and yet on earth? What is he now, then? If he was such when imprisoned in the flesh, what is he now in the full liberty and largeness of his heavenly state?"

How hateful is that religion which says, "Business is business, and politics are politics, and religion is religion"! Religion is using every thing for God; but many men dedicate business to the devil, and politics to the devil, and shove religion into the cracks and crevices of time, and make it the hypocritical outcrawling of their leisure and laziness.

As sometimes, when we go to our work in summer, we are annoyed by swarms of insects that fill the air with murmurous buzz, and trouble the eye and the ear, and offend every sense, so there are some passages in the Bible so infested by commentators, by controversialists, and theologians, and curious Christians, that one cannot approach them except through a swarm of buzzing associations which distract the reason, and pervert the judgment, and take away all the heart enjoyment which they were meant to give. The only way to get at the truth is to strip them of all foregone knowledges. Among these passages is the eighth chapter of Romans, which one would think was a grindstone on which all men sharpened their wits, and brought their theories to an edge and a point. Do not read this chapter with commentaries; if you do, they will raise such a dust that you cannot see a foot before you. It is going over Jordan into the promised land to read this chapter as it was intended to be read. I could walk over it dry-shod, as the Israelites did over the Red Sea. It is only those who are wise in their head, and poverty-stricken in their heart, upon whom the waves of difficulty return on either side. It was meant to open up the regality of God's nature, and to show his bounteous love and tenderness towards those "who are the called according to his purpose" — that is, who *love* him.

THE boy holds his ball of twine in his hand, and thinks it is not much, he can clasp it so easily; but when he begins to unroll it, and his wind-borne kite mounts higher and higher, till, at length, that which, on the ground, was taller than he, is now no bigger than his hand, he is astonished to see how long it is. So there are little texts which look small in your palm, but when caught up upon some experience, they unfold themselves, and stretch out until there is no measuring their length.

I HAVE always been much affected by Christ's reply to the Syro-Phœnician woman, when she begged him to cast the devil out of her daughter. If I saw the poorest child in the street falling down in convulsions, and agonized and distorted with pain, and it were in my power to restore her, how gladly would I go to her, and raise her up, and bring her back to health and joy! Now, how little is my willingness, compared to Christ's! for what in me is one little pulsation, in him is the tide of the universe. His heart went out towards the poor suppliant with infinite yearning and tenderness. He longed, and meant, to grant her request, and yet he stops to parley with her: "It is not meet to take the children's bread, and to cast it unto the dogs." I hardly know how to express this delaying of mercy in God — this sublime playfulness, is it? — this coyness, is not that the word? or is it a certain holding back, as one draws the bow back when he means to send the shaft yet farther?

The apostle speaks of things which are not, as bringing to nought things that are; and so many of Christ's silences impress me full as much as his sayings; his rests and not-doings seem even more significant, at times, than that which was overt. That which he said was what could be expressed and received by the mind; but when, pausing, he said, "I have yet many things to say unto you, but ye cannot bear them now," my imagination is inflamed as with the idea of an upper sphere too vast for words or interpretation.

Many Christians are like chestnuts — very pleasant nuts, but enclosed in very prickly burs, which need various dealings of Nature, and her grip of frost, before the kernel is disclosed.

In moist and liberal summers, the wheat is often covered with fungi and parasitic plants; and it has to be put through smutting machines, that it may be cleansed, and made ready for grinding into flour. So men, in prosperity, often have fungi and parasitic plants growing on almost every faculty; and then, to purify them, God puts them through trials which are like smutting machines to the wheat. The best thing which can happen to such men is a trouble that will bolt them.

As a general rule, self-contemplation is a power towards mischief. The only way to grow is to look out of one's self. There is too much introversion among Christians. A shipmaster might as well look down into the hold of his ship for the north star, as a Christian look down into his own heart for the sun of righteousness. Out and beyond is the shining.

As I grow older, and come nearer to death, I look upon it more and more with complacent joy, and out of every longing I hear God say, "O thirsting, hungering one, come to me." What the other life will bring I know not, only that I shall awake in God's likeness, and see him as he is. If a child had been born and spent all his life in the Mammoth Cave, how impossible would it be for him to comprehend the upper world! His parents might tell him of its life, and light, and beauty, and its sounds of joy; they might heap up the sand into mounds, and try to show him by pointing to stalactites how grass, and flowers, and trees grow out of the ground, till at length, with laborious thinking, the child would fancy he had gained a true idea of the unknown land. And yet, though he longed to behold it, when the day came that he was to go forth, it would be with regret for the familiar crystals, and the rock-hewn rooms, and the quiet that reigned therein. But when he came up, some May morning, with ten thousand birds singing in the trees, and the heavens bright, and blue, and full of sunlight, and the wind blowing softly through the young leaves, all a-glitter with dew, and the landscape stretching away green and beautiful to the horizon, with what rapture would he gaze about him, and see how poor were all the fancyings and the interpretations which were made within the cave, of the things which grew and lived without; and how would he wonder that he could have regretted to leave the silence and the dreary darkness of his old abode! So, when we emerge from this cave of earth into that land where spring growths are, and where is summer, and not that miserable travestie which we call summer here, how shall we wonder that we could have clung so fondly to this dark and barren life!

Beat on, then, O heart, and yearn for dying. I have drunk at many a fountain, but thirst came again; I have fed at many a bounteous table, but hunger returned; I have seen many bright and lovely things, but, while I gazed, their lustre faded. There is nothing here that can give me rest; but when I behold thee, O God, I shall be satisfied!

It is a joy to me to know that the Christians within the communion of this church are not all the Christians to be found in the congregation. We are richer than we appear to be. Here are growing pear trees, apple trees, cherry trees, and shrubs, and blossoming vines, and flowers of every hue and odor; but I am glad that some seeds have been blown over the wall, and that fruit trees and flowers most pleasant to the eye are springing up there also. And though I wish they were within the enclosure, where the boar out of the wood could not waste them, and the wild beast of the field devour them, yet I love them, and am glad to see them growing there. To all such I say, God nourish and protect you, and bring you, with us, to the garden above.

A man may look over an artist at his work, and see that he makes bad strokes, but yet shall see that he is *to be* a good artist. The sense of his purpose is not marred by his imperfect execution. So a Christian may have an irritable temper, or be a proud man, and yet may live so that the impression is produced that he is trying to regulate his interior nature by the law of Christ. He is a Christian who is manfully struggling to live a Christian's life.

REASON can tell how love affects us, but cannot tell what love is.

DID you ever sit in a half-cleared forest, in a summer's day, and, looking up, see the light come fleckering down in uncounted shades of golden brown and greenish gold, and these all the while changing and running into each other with the rustling leaves and the cloud-crossed sun? How useless to attempt to chronicle this play and interplay of light and dark! yet this would be simple and easy, compared with the effort to note the number and variety of our thoughts and feelings for a single hour. If the flow of a day's mind and heart experiences were written, it would be a volume, and one's life a Bodleian library; but the "book of remembrance" is yonder, and the life is daguerreotyped on the sensitive pages of the future.

As ships meet at sea, a moment together, when words of greeting must be spoken, and then away upon the deep, so men meet in this world; and I think we should cross no man's path without hailing him, and, if he needs, giving him supplies.

THREE natural philosophers go out into the forest and find a nightingale's nest, and forthwith they begin to discuss the habits of the bird, its size, its color, and the number of eggs it lays; and one pulls out of his pocket a treatise of Buffon, and another of Cuvier, and another of Audubon, and they read and dispute till at length the quarrel runs so high over the empty nest, that they tear each other's leaves, and get red in the face, and the woods ring with their conflict; when, lo! out of the green shade of a neighboring thicket, the bird itself, rested, and disturbed by these side noises, begins to sing. At first its song is soft and low, and then it rises and swells, and waves of melody float up over the trees, and fill the air with tremulous music, and all the forest doth hush; and the entranced philosophers, subdued and ashamed of their quarrel, shut their books and walk home without a word.

So men who around the empty sepulchre of Christ have wrangled about the forms of religion, about creeds, and doctrines, and ordinances, when Christ himself, disturbed by their discords, sings to them, out of heaven, of love, and peace, and joy in the Holy Ghost, are ashamed of their conflicts, and go quietly and meekly to their duties.

THERE are some men who are so outrageously cultivated, that they are miserable the moment they are away from all which is exquisite. It is a pity that such men were born into a rough world like this, where God forgot to finish up rocks, and to make tree-trunks smooth, and to slope the mountains down gently to the plains. That is true cultivation which gives us sympathy with every form of human life, and enables us to work most successfully for its advancement. Refinement that carries us away from our fellow-men is not God's refinement.

IF a boy is not trained to endure and to bear trouble, he will grow up a girl; and a boy that is a girl has all a girl's weakness without any of her regal qualities. A woman made out of a woman is God's noblest work; a woman made out of a man is his meanest. A child rightly brought up will be like a willow branch, which, broken off and touching the ground, at once takes root. Bring up your children so that they will root easily in their own soil, and not forever be grafted into your old trunk and boughs.

As, in freshets on western rivers, sticks of timber and broken branches are borne down the flood and lodged in the boughs of trees, where they remain for years, lifted far up above the ground, dry and helpless, so, in revival freshets, men are sometimes caught in the boughs of this or that church, and stay merely because they are lodged there; and men passing by afterwards, and seeing dry logs strangely perched in so uncouth a way, wonder what force of water ever bore such worthless stuff so high.

A CHRISTIAN merchant should so act that his customers shall see and know that he is a Christian; not merely that he conducts his business on great maxims of honesty, but that business itself is subordinate and instrumental to the great purposes of life. Is it so with you? How far does the difference between you and the worldly man lie in the fact, that on the seventh day you have a little tabernacle of religious experience into which you run? Go through the streets and stores of New York;

you can pick out the men that are wealthy; can you pick out the men that are Christians? What wonder that truth makes such slow advances in the world, with one Christian to tell what is true for two hours on Sunday, and hundreds to deny it all the week by their lives!

MANY men are lamenting their misfortunes, and wishing that their place was changed that they might the more easily live Christianly. If a man cannot be a Christian in the place where he is, he cannot be a Christian any where.

IF I could not send a man among the mountains, or through the valleys, or by the side of streams, I would shut him up in the resounding recesses of the Old Testament. There is more loving description of nature in the Psalms alone, than in all Greek and Roman literature. Yet the Bible has been used so unfairly, and a truckling priesthood have drawn from it such base arguments, that men of free and generous natures have been repelled by it, and have gone away with the wings of literature and the feet of science to find God in the great realm of nature. In those sciences which might be called the light infantry of progress, the Zouaves of thought, that are skirmishing in the valleys, and hanging along the hills, and sending vanguards against the enemy, there is much infidelity.

I, too, will go out and read God in the strata; I, too, through the stars will hear the chiming of the spheres; I will be behind none in enjoying the sweet perfume of flowers; but when I do all this, I will remember that the Bible is the beacon fire at which I have lighted the torch that has guided me to this knowledge and these delights.

A CONSERVATIVE young man has wound up his life before it was unreeled. We expect old men to be conservative, but when a nation's young men are so, its funeral bell is already rung.

WHERE is there a reason strong enough to fly up and pluck the secret out of the bosom of God, which it has not pleased his tongue to make known? I accept the fact, the simple fact, the august, solemn fact, that it was necessary for Christ to suffer; the theological explanations I do not believe a word in.

Those who say that Christ's sufferings were not vicarious, will have to fight, not only with the Bible, but with all the weight of human life. Suffering, in human life, is very widely vicarious. Every man feels this in himself, one part of his being paying another's penalty. If he loves overmuch, it is not love that suffers, but conscientiousness. If his passions are unduly excited, it is his moral nature that feels the transgression. If the brain be overwrought, the body feels it. The first lesson of life is one of vicarious suffering. As we go to the ship to see friends depart, and leave them with cheers, and benedictions, and wafted kisses, so when a young spirit is about to be launched into this earthly life, one would think that troops of angels would attend it, and with hope and gladness see it on its way. But no. Silently it passes the bounds of the unseen land, and the gate which opens to admit it to this, is a gate of tears and moans. Through the sorrow of another is it ushered into existence. Love cannot clasp all it yearns for, in its bosom, without first suffering for it. The child lives upon its parents' life. The child which has no one to suffer for it is a miserable wretch. And, from this point onward, in every relation of life, one man suffers for another's benefit. It is the law of social life, and I do not see why we should think it strange that Christ obeyed the same law, only in a grander way.

Consecration is not wrapping one's self in a holy web in the sanctuary, and then coming forth after prayer and twilight meditation, and saying, "There, I am consecrated." Consecration is going out into the world where God Almighty is, and using every power for his glory. It is taking all advantages as trust funds — as confidential debts owed to God. It is simply dedicating one's life, in its whole flow, to God's service.

There is nothing which the world resents so much as an attempt to carry out a better measure than existed before. A man who would benefit the world must take leave of his own reputation first; for the world never let a man bless it but it first fought him; it never let him give it a boon without first giving him a buffet. If with one effort you should raise a tree twenty feet high, so as to make it forty feet high, you would not do more violence to its roots than you do to society, when you attempt suddenly to elevate it above its former level. If there were a hundred violins together, all playing below concert pitch, and I should take a real Cremona, and with the hand of a Paganini should bring it strongly up to the true key, and then should sweep my bow across it like a storm, and make it sound forth clear and resonant, what a demoniac jargon would the rest of the playing seem! Yet the other musicians would be enraged at me. They would think all the discord was mine, and I should be to them a demoniac. So it is with reformers. The world thinks the discord is with them, and not in its own false playing. All those rosy philosophers who go dancing along the ways of life, and expect to reform men through ease and pleasure, and are surprised when at first snow flakes are thrown at them, and then icicles, and then avalanches, had better fold their gauzy wings at once. They are not wanted. They are not of that heroic race who advance the world.

HEART knowledge, through God's teaching, is true wealth, and they are often poorest who deem themselves most rich. I, in the pulpit, preach with loud words to many a humble widow and stricken man who might well teach me. The student, spectacled and gray with wisdom, and stuffed with lumbered lore, may be childish and ignorant beside some old singing saint who carries the wood into his study, and who, with the lens of his own experience, brings down the orbs of truth, and beholds, through his faith and his humility, things of which the white-haired scholar never dreamed.

CHRIST took the part of religion against religious institutions; of religious feeling against religious usages, which are often venerable, in proportion as they are nothing else. God's law of love, which the Jews had made stone, was smitten by Christ, and made to gush with water for the poor that lay athirst and gasping in the dust.

No matter how infidel philosophers may regard the Bible; they may say that Genesis is awry, and that the Psalms are more than half bitter imprecations, and the Prophecies only the fantasies of brain-bewildered men, and the Gospels weak laudations of an impostor, and the Epistles but the letters of a mad Jew, and that the whole book has had its day; I shall cling to it until they show me a better revelation. The Bible emptied, effete, worn out! If all the wisest men of the world were placed man to man, they could not sound the shallowest depth of the Gospel of John. O philosophers! break the shell, and fly out, and let me hear how you can sing. Not of passion — I know that already; not of worldly power — I hear that every where; but teach me, through your song, how to find joy in sorrow, strength in weakness, and light in darkest days; how to bear buffeting and scorn, how to welcome death, and to pass through its ministration into the sphere of life; and this, not for me only, but for the whole world that groans and travails in pain; and until you can do this, speak not to me of a better revelation.

THE great ocean is in a constant state of evaporation. It gives back what it receives, and sends up its waters in mists to gather into clouds; and so there is rain on the fields, and storm on the mountains, and greenness and beauty every where. But there are many men who do not believe in evaporation. They get all they can and keep all they get, and so are not fertilizers, but only stagnant, miasmatic pools.

AN acorn is not an oak tree when it is sprouted. It must go through long summers and fierce winters; it has to endure all that frost, and snow, and thunder, and storm, and side-striking winds can bring, before it is a full-grown oak. These are rough teachers; but, rugged schoolmasters make rugged pupils. So a man is not a man when he is created — he is only begun. His manhood must come with years. A man who goes through life prosperous, and comes to his grave without a wrinkle, is not half a man. In time of war, whom does the general select for some hazardous enterprise? He looks over his men, and chooses the soldier whom he knows will not flinch at danger, but will go bravely through whatever is allotted to him. He calls him that he may receive his orders, and the officer, blushing with pleasure to be thus chosen, hastens away to execute them. Difficulties are God's errands. And when we are sent upon them we should esteem it a proof of God's confidence — as a compliment from God. The traveller who goes round the world prepares himself to pass through all latitudes, and to meet all changes. So a man must be willing to take life as it comes; to mount the hill when the hill swells, and to go down the hill when the hill lowers; to walk the plain when it stretches before him, and to ford the river when it rolls over the plain. "I can do all things through Christ which strengtheneth me."

THERE is no harder shield for the devil to pierce with temptation than singing with prayer.

IF the architect of a house had one plan, and the contractor had another, what conflicts would there be! How many walls would have to come down, how many doors and windows would need to be altered, before the two could harmonize! Of the building of life, God is the Architect, and man is the contractor. God has one plan, and man has another. Is it strange that there are clashings and collisions?

THINKING is creating, with God, as thinking is writing, with the ready writer; and worlds are only leaves turned over in the process of composition, about his throne.

OUR sweetest experiences of affection are meant to be suggestions of that realm which is the home of the heart.

RELIGION, in one sense, is a life of self-denial, just as husbandry, in one sense, is a work of death. You go and bury a seed, and that is husbandry; but you bury one that you may reap a hundred fold. Self-denial does not belong to religion as characteristic of it; it belongs to human life. The lower nature must always be denied when you are trying to rise to a higher sphere. It is no more necessary to be self-denying to be a Christian, than it is to be an artist, or to be an honest man, or to be a man at all, in distinction from a brute. Of all joyful, smiling, ever-laughing experiences, there are none like those which spring from true religion. "When the Lord turned again the captivity of Zion, then was our mouth filled with laughter."

THE apostle says, "Now unto Him that is able to do exceeding abundantly, above all that we can ask or think." What a vision he must have had! How grandly in that moment did the divine thought rise before his enrapt mind when he so linked words together — joining golden word to golden word, as if he fain would encompass it with a chain, seeking by combinations to express what no one word could embody! "Above all that we can ask or think!" How much can a man ask or think? When the deepest convictions of sin are upon him, in his hour of dark despondency, in some perilous pass of life, when fears come upon his soul as storms on the Lake Galilee, consider how much a man then *asks!* Or when love swells in his soul, and makes life as full as mountains make the streams in spring, and hope is the sun by day and the moon by night, — in those gloriously elate hours when he seems no longer fixed to space and time, but, mounting as if the body were forgotten by the soul, wings his way through the realm of aspiration and conception, consider how much a man then *thinks!* All books are dry and tame compared with the great unwritten book uttered in the closet. The prayers of exiles, of martyrs, of missionaries, of the Waldenses, of the Covenanters, of mothers for children gone astray, when with plash of tears, and yearnings that can find no speech, they implore God's mercy upon them, — if some angel, catching them as they were uttered, should drop them down from heaven, what a liturgy would they make! What epic can equal those *unwritten* words which pour into the ear of God out of the heart's fulness! still more, those *unspoken* words which never find the lip, but go up to heaven in unutterable longings and aspirations! Words are but the bannerets of a great army, a few bits of waving color here and there; thoughts are the main body of the footmen that march unseen below. Words cannot follow thoughts and feelings even in their tamer flights, still less when they take wings and soar towards God. Every day, from my window, I see the gulls making circuits and beating against the north wind. Now they mount high above the masts of vessels in the stream, and then suddenly drop to the water's edge, seeking to find some eddy unobstructed by the steady-blowing blast; till, at length, abandoning their efforts, they turn and fly with the wind; and then how like a gleam of light do their white wings flash down the bay faster than eye can follow! So, when we cease to resist God's divine influences, and, turning towards him, our thoughts and feelings are upborne by the breath of his spirit, how do they make such swift heavenward flight as no words can overtake!

Yet, wonderful as are the desires and thoughts of the soul, the apostle's measurement is more than these; for he says, "Now unto Him that is able to do exceeding abundantly, above all that we *ask or think!*" Truly his riches are unsearchable.

If we dwelt more upon God's fulness, and his desire to make us partakers of it, our Christian character would be richer. God never reveals himself to us as a distant, glimmering light. Of all stars he calls himself "the bright and morning star"—the star that lingers longest in the sky, and swims and glorifies an *avant courier* of the sun, as John the Baptist did in the rising splendor of Christ. Many people get a wrong idea of God by thinking of him as infinite only in justice and power; but infinite applies to the feelings of God, as much as to the stretch of his right hand. There is nothing in his nature which is not measureless. Many think God sits brooding in heaven, as storms brood in summer skies, full of bolts and rain, and believe that they must come to him under the covert of some apology, or beneath some umbrellaed excuse, lest the clouds should break, and the tempest overwhelm them. But when men repent towards God, they go not to storms, but to serene and tranquil skies, and to a Father who waits to receive them with all tenderness, and delicacy, and love. His eye is not dark with vengeance, nor his heart turbulent with wrath; and to repent towards his justice and vindictiveness must always be from a lower motive than to repent towards his generosity and love.

This view of God's plenitude, habitually taken, will deliver us from unworthy fears, and enable us with confidence to approach his throne. It will give us hope of rectitude in life, and of glorification in heaven; not because of our feeble longing, but because of God's infinite desire for us. When stars, first created, start forth upon their vast circuits, not knowing their way, if they were conscious and sentient, they might feel hopeless of maintaining their revolutions and orbits, and despair in the face of coming ages. But, without hands or arms, the sun holds them. Without cords or bands the solar king drives them unharnessed on their mighty rounds without a single misstep, and will bring them, in the end, to their bound without a wanderer. Now, if the sun can do this, the sun, which is but a thing, itself driven and held, shall not He who created the heavens, and gave the sun his power, be able to hold *us* by the attraction of his heart, the strength of his hands, and the omnipotence of his affectionate will?

But some will say, "Such views will lead to Universalism." Does Matthew teach this? Does Mark, or Luke, or John teach it? Do they say, "To be sure God is a God of love, but take care that you do not presume upon it?" No. The first, and second, and third view of God is love. Justice is alternative. He has conscience and integrity, and he must preserve the rectitude of his kingdom; but love is his abiding place. When men were almost animals, fear was employed to bring them to God; but when they were driven a certain way towards right, then God sent higher influences to act upon them. He gave his Son to die for the world; and a thousand men will be drawn by Calvary, where one will approach through the terrors of Sinai. The New Testament opens with, "Peace on earth, good will to men;" and these were the last words that rung through the air before the vision faded: "And the Spirit and the bride say, Come; and let him that heareth say, Come; and let him that is athirst come; and whosoever will, let him come and drink of the water of life freely;" and all between these two magnificent notes rolls the anthem of God's mercy. "*Whosoever will!*" That is the beginning and the ending. Let every Christian heart respond in those final and sublimest words of revelation, "Even so, come, Lord Jesus!"

FLOWERS are the sweetest things that God ever made, and forgot to put a soul into.

FAR in the woods of Maine, in these winter months, there are a hundred camps, and scores of axemen are busy cutting down the huge trees, and measuring the logs, and sorting them, and throwing them into deep gullies, where they will lie dry and undisturbed until the snows melt, and the spring floods come, and then they will be borne out of the ravines into the ever deep-flowing river, and from thence to some Penobscot or Kennebec, and there collected together, and bound in mighty rafts, they will float down to tide waters. So men are lying, dry logs along empty channels, hoping that some revival freshet will come and sweep them down to deep waters of piety.

IT is not desirable that we should live as in the constant atmosphere and presence of death; that would unfit us for life; but it is well for us, now and then, to talk with death as friend talketh with friend, and to bathe in the strange seas, and to anticipate the experiences of that land to which it will lead us. These forethinkings are meant, not to make us discontented with life, but to bring us back with more strength, and a nobler purpose in living. A banner long unused, and laid away in a dark chamber, grows dusty and moth eaten, and needs, for its preservation, to be unrolled and shaken out, and borne high in air: so our spiritual life decays in the confinement and darkness of the world; and that it may gain new vigor, our thoughts must now and then be unfurled, and held high, and shaken in the air of heaven.

A MAN who emigrates from the low country of selfishness, where are perpetual chills and fevers, to the high lands of benevolence, goes from sickness and barrenness to the realm of health, and plenty, and joy, where his hand can almost pluck the fruits from the tree of life itself.

SUFFERING, in repentance, is not in itself meritorious; it is only instrumental. Many persons aim at suffering as a mode of producing a change of heart; but this is the monkish idea of bodily torture for penance. Old warriors, whose lives had been spent in crime and self-indulgence, saw some vision, some stag in the woods with a cross between his horns, and forthwith they were frightened, and resolved to amend their ways, and clothed themselves in haircloth, and were miserable the rest of their days to atone for the sins of their youth. Now, our asceticism has gone beyond this. It does not relate to the body, but to the mind. One who in youth has strayed from virtue, never forgets his error, but checks every smile with, "you remember," and lets gall from the old bitterness exude on every flower of pleasure. This is not God's example. He says, if we turn from sin he will make no mention of our transgressions, and our iniquities he will remember no more. So, when we have heartily repented of wrong, we should let all the waves of forgetfulness roll over it, and go forward unburdened to meet the future. "Forgetting those things which are behind, and reaching forth unto those things which are before, I press towards the mark for the prize of the high calling of God in Christ Jesus."

A LOW and normal action of fear leads to forecast; its morbid action is a positive hinderance to effort. Water is necessary for the floating of timber; but if a log be saturated with water, it sinks in the very element which should buoy it up. Many men are water-logged with anxiety, and instead of quickening them, it only paralyzes exertion.

MORALITY is character and conduct, such as is required by the circle or community in which the man's life happens to be placed. It shows how much good *men* require of us. Religion is the endeavor of a man with all his mind, and heart, and soul, to form his life and his character upon the true elements of love and submission to God, and love and good will to man. A spiritual Christian is like a man who learns the principles of music, and then goes on to the practice. A moralist is like a man who learns nothing of the principles, but only a few airs by rote, and is satisfied to know as many tunes as common people do. Morality is good, and is accepted of God, as far as it goes; but the difficulty is, it does not go far enough. "Is not my fifty fathom cable as good as your hundred fathom one?" says the sailor. Yes, as far as it goes; but in water a hundred fathoms deep, if it does not go within fifty fathoms of anchorage, of what use will it be in a storm?

The Christian and the moralist are alike in many things, but by and by the Christian will be admitted to a sphere which the moralist cannot enter. A barren and a fruitful vine are growing side by side in the garden, and the barren vine says to the fruitful one, —

"Is not my root as good as yours?"

"Yes," replies the vine, "as good as mine."

"And are not my lower leaves as broad and spreading, and is not my stem as large, and my bark as shaggy?"

"Yes," says the vine.

"And are not my leaves as green, and have I not as many bugs creeping up and down, and am I not taller than you?"

"Yes," meekly replies the vine, "but I have blossoms."

"O! blossoms are of no use."

"But I bear fruit."

"What, those clusters? Those are only a trouble to a vine."

But what thinks the vintner? He passes by the barren vine; but the other, filling the air with its odor in spring, and drooping with purple clusters in autumn, is his pride and joy; and he lingers near it, and prunes it that it may become yet more luxuriant and fruitful. So the moralist and the Christian may grow together for a while; but by and by, when the moralist's life is barren, the Christian's will come to flower and fruitage in the garden of God. "Herein is my Father glorified, that ye bear much fruit."

THERE are few complete loves on earth. Though thousands love, and earnestly, yet no one knows the whole want of his life till he has met that which is a supply to all — mind to mind, heart to heart, faculty to faculty. But the supply is so scanty, and man is so poor! It is only God who can satisfy the soul.

WE bury men when they are dead, but we try to embalm the dead body of laws, keeping the corpse in sight long after the vitality has gone. It usually takes a hundred years to make a law; and then, after it has done its work, it usually takes a hundred years to get rid of it. When we have gained our health, we do not repeat the portion of medicine, but we keep on dosing with law when the evil which it was meant to cure has passed away.

NOTHING which comes into the world in the way of divine truth is ever lost. You may open your cage and let your singing bird fly out, and he may wander away, and the song he sang you may never hear in your home again; but when God opens the door of heaven, and lets some singing truth, angel-winged, fly down to earth, it is never lost, but one catches the strain here, and another repeats it there, till at length it becomes choral.

The truth may change its form; it may be hid for years and generations; but, as the old wheat seeds, wrapped in the mummies of Egypt, now, after ages, sought out by prying travellers and planted, are found not to have lost their germ, but to have kept it through the sleep of three thousand years, so God's truths, hid in dead forms and institutions, slumbering in the grave of old books and libraries, or banished from polite society to live in the rags of the vulgar, do at length come forth with unimpaired germ, losing no more by their burial than did Christ, their Master. Like him they carry an unquenched heart through the grave. They bring forth light from its darkness, and in spite of brute force and watchful authority, they stand again upon the earth, and look abroad with eyes of immortality.

HEATHENISM was always exalting the top of society, the great men, and taking no thought for the masses below them. Christianity says, "The great and the strong can take care of themselves," and so seeks to elevate the lowest and poorest. Christ never warned us against not respecting a king's crown; but his words were, "Whoso shall offend one of these little ones which believe in me, it were better for him that a millstone were hanged about his neck, and that he were drowned in the depth of the sea." As in the family, it is not the son of twenty-one years, but the babe, whom the mother rocks to sleep in the cradle, so, in Christ's family of earth, it is not the full-grown and the mature for whom he most tenderly provides; it is the weak, and those on whom the world's law tramples, that he takes tenderly up with his strong arm, and rocks in the cradle of his love and care.

THE elect are whosoever will, and the non-elect whosoever won't.

THE growth of Christian life is to be measured by the growth of *love;* and love itself is to be measured in its progressive states by its restfulness, its undisturbed trust, its victory over every form of fear. The state of perfect loving is incompatible with distrust. When the heart is first awakened to affection, it is disturbed and agitated. It fluctuates with every shade of hope and fear alternately. It rushes from one extreme of confidence to the opposite of doubt. But this is only while it is *filling*. The heart beginning to love is like a bay into which the star-drawn tides are rushing. The waters come with violence. They stir up the sand and sediment. They dash and murmur on the edges of the shore. They whirl and chafe about the rocks, and the whole bay is agitated with strife and counter-strife of swirling waters, until they have nearly reached their height. Then, when great depth is gained, when the shores are full, when no more room is found for the floods, the bay begins to tranquillize itself, to clear its surface; and effacing every wrinkle, and blowing out every bubble, and hushing every ripple along the shore, it looks up with an open and tranquil face into the sky, and reflects clearly the sun and moon that have drawn it thither. And so does the soul, while filling, whirl with disquiet, and fret its edges with wrinkles and eddies; but when it is filled with love, it rests and looks calmly up, and reflects the image of its God!

THE truths of the Bible are like gold in the soil. Whole generations walk over it, and know not what treasures are hidden beneath. So centuries of men pass over the Scriptures, and know not what riches lie under the feet of their interpretation. Sometimes, when they discover them, they call them new truths. One might as well call gold, newly dug, new gold.

God is a being who gives every thing but punishment in over measure. The whole divine character and administration, the whole conception of God as set forth in the Bible and in nature, is of a being of munificence, of abundance and superabundance. Enough is a measuring word — a sufficiency and no more; economy, not profusion. God never deals in this way. With him there is always a magnificent overplus. The remotest corner of the globe is full of wonder and beauty. The laziest bank in the world, away from towns, where no artists do congregate, upon which no farm laps, where no vines hang their cooling clusters, nor flowers spring, nor grass invites the browsing herd, is yet spotted and patched with moss of such exquisite beauty, that the painter who in all his life should produce one such thing would be a master in art and immortal in fame, and it has the hair of ten thousand reeds combed over its brow, and its shining sand and insect tribes might win the student's lifetime.

God's least thought is more prolific than man's greatest abundance.

At first babes feed on the mother's bosom, but always on her heart.

All the might of the world is now on the side of Christianity. Those barbarous, inchoate powers which still cling to heathenism, are already trembling before the advancing strides of the Christian nations; Christian just enough to rouse all their energies, and to make them intensely ambitious and on the alert to increase their own dominion, without having learned Christianity's highest lesson, the lesson of love.

Even that heathenism which seems to have some power, is only waiting for its time of decay. In vast, undisturbed forests, whose intertwining boughs exclude the light, moisture is generated, and rills, fed by marshes and quiet pools, unite to form running rivers. But let the trees be cut down, and the ground be laid open to the sun, and the swamps will dry up, and the rivers run no more. So is it with the Brahmins, and with all the effete teachers of heathenism. As long as the dense shadows of ignorance brood over the people, they will possess some little trickling power; but let the light of knowledge shine in upon the masses, and the channels of their influence will dry up and be forgotten.

Already, war, with its bloody hand, raps at the gate of empire in India and in China. England presses upon them. Russia is steadily moving through craunching snows to the southward. The great nations, like lions roused from their lairs, are roaring and springing upon the prey, and the little nations, like packs of hungry wolves, are standing by, licking their jaws, and waiting for their share of the spoils. The world is out hunting — what? Heathenism. And it will be caught; it will be unearthed. A little while and there will be no den so deep, or forest so dark, or island so remote, that it can find refuge.

CONCEITED men often seem a harmless kind of men, who, by an overweening self-respect, relieve others from the duty of respecting them at all.

IN my schoolboy drawing lessons, when I came to the human face, my master gave me first the eyes to practise upon, and then the nose, and then the mouth, and then the ears, and then the brow and hair, and after long weeks the day came when I was to combine them. I knew where to set the eyes, one over against the other, where to draw down the nose, and to open the mouth, and to place the ears, and to shade the hair about the forehead; and so, at last, I had a perfect face. Now, God is the great draught-master, and the world is his pupil. Here and there, through laws and institutions, he is developing the single features, and at length the day will come when they shall be combined to form a perfect manhood in Christ Jesus.

At the Military Academy, the soldiers are taken separately to the drill room, and there the martinet puts them through all the steps, and passes, and gestures, which they are required to learn; and when they have been trained and disciplined, they come to the parade ground; and then, at the word of command, platoons march, and squadrons wheel, and the great army, as one man, moves to the voice of its leader. Now, God's formative influences in this world are his military academies, his drill rooms, where for centuries the soldiers of the cross have been trained; but the day is coming when he shall put to his lips the trumpet of announcement, and when, with uplifted standard and triumphal music, he shall lead forth his vast army to go round and round the world with victory!

How in the household are garments quilted, and wrought, and curiously embroidered, and the softest things laid aside, and the cradle prepared to greet the little pilgrim of love when it comes from distant regions, we know not whence. Now, no cradle for an emperor's child was ever prepared with such magnificence as this world has been for man. It is God's cradle for the race; curiously carved and decorated, flower-strewn and star-curtained. But because it is the cradle, and because we are yet in our infancy, God had not scope to give himself expression. What is to come we know not. "Eye hath not seen, nor ear heard, neither have entered into the heart of man, the things which God hath prepared for them that love him."

As prisoners in castles look out of their grated windows at the smiling landscape where the sun comes and goes, so we, from this life, as from dungeon bars, look forth to the heavenly land, and are refreshed with sweet visions of the home that shall be ours when we are free.

Christ declared without qualification, "I am the light of the world." What thunderous strokes should beat down the audacious man who should dare to say this! If Christ had not been the absolute one, he would have said, "I am the moon, shining by night, but my spoused one, the sun, from whom I receive my beams, shines by day."

Again: "If any man thirst, let him come unto me and drink." What man would dare to say of merely physical things, "If any man lacks knowledge, let him come to me." Neither Humboldt, nor Liebig, nor Agassiz would dare to say this, even of the departments in which they are preëminent, how much less of the whole range of learning! yet Christ, disdaining physical things, appeals at once to the soul with all its yearnings, its depths of despair, its claspings, — like a mother feeling at midnight for the child whom death has taken, — its infinite outreachings, its longings for love, and peace, and joy, which nothing can satisfy this side of the bosom of God, and says, "If any man thirst, let him come unto me and drink." He stands over against whatever want there is in the human bosom, whatever hunger there is in the moral faculties, whatever need there is in the imagination, and says, "He that cometh to me shall never hunger, and he that believeth on me shall never thirst."

There is no heresy in the long list of heresies which have invaded the church, like the heresy of negativeness, of inaction, of death. The dead man is the great heresiarch.

Nowhere in the Bible is it said, "Give Christ what is due to him, but leave some store for God when you reach heaven." On the contrary, we are pressed, we are urged, we are crowded, we are touched by the Bible on every hand, as summer soil is by summer sun, to spring forth in all growths, both high and low, and to give them all into the bosom of the Lord Jesus Christ. Should a vine wind its thousand tendrils round a trellis, its life would be destroyed if they were rudely cut and torn away. Now, the soul has more tendrils than any climbing vine, and if they have all clung about the Lord Jesus as their divine support, how worse than death will it be to wake up in the awful judgment to find that he is but a creature, and to be wrenched forever from him! If Christ be not God, then to worship him is idolatry, and the Father has deluded and deceived the world.

O Lord Jesus! My heart cries out from its depths that thou art very God. In thee I find rest and satisfaction. Thy heart opens like summer to one who navigates from high northern latitudes, and takes me into its tropical embrace. All thoughts and feelings that rise, singing, in my soul, fly home to thee as birds to their nests. And thy stores are infinite. When the mother tires of the child, and puts it away from the bosom where it draws its sweet life; when the friend who has yearned for love says to the loving one, "Enough, I am sated;" when the soul that has known only dreary wastes of experience, having come at last to a realm of song and bloom, calls back the darkness and the desert; even then, O Lord, I shall not weary of thee! But where in my heart there is one drop of affection, I would increase it till it should be as the unmeasured ocean; where now I look at thee with adoring eyes, I would multiply my glances till my face should glow as does the sky when night reveals the stars; I would dedicate myself to thee — various, universal, total self — to thee, my King and my God!

There are many professing Christians who are secretly vexed on account of the charity they have to bestow, and the self-denial they have to use. If, instead of the smooth prayers which they *do* pray, they should speak out the things which they really feel, they would say, when they go home at night,

"O Lord, I met a poor wretch of yours to-day, a miserable, unwashed brat, and I gave him sixpence, and I have been sorry for it ever since;" or, "O Lord, if I had not signed those articles of faith, I might have gone to the theatre this evening. Your religion deprives me of a great deal of enjoyment; but I mean to stick to it. There's no other way of getting into heaven, I suppose."

The sooner such men are out of the church, the better.

IF, every time conscience was wronged, it sighed, and every time reason was perverted, it uttered complaints, no one could live for the moaning which would fill his soul.

SOME men, when they attempt to reform their lives, reform those things for which they do not much care. They take the torch of God's word, and enter some indifferent chamber, and the light blazes in, and they see that they are very sinful there; and then they look into another room, where they do not often stay, and are willing to admit that they are very sinful there; but they leave unexplored some cupboards and secret apartments where their life really is, and where they have stored up the things which are dearest to them, and which they will neither part from, nor suffer rebuke for.

THE young, who recoil from impositions, sometimes say, "I have no proof of invisible things. I will believe in nothing which my reason does not show me."

The differences between men lie in their power and scope of rising above the senses into the region of the invisible. All men in action, if not in profession, recognize this life beyond the senses. The material man says, "I believe in nothing which I cannot see," and so he goes about collecting facts from observation. But what does he do with them? He sublimes them into a principle, and that is invisible.

You may unscrew and take off the end of a telescope, and you will have only a magnifying glass with which you can examine the objects about you. Return it to its place, and new powers will be added to it, and things which are remote will begin to lift themselves with marvellous clarity. Draw out the tube, and you can pierce yet farther the distance, till at length your vision sweeps the stellar universe. Now, we can employ our reason upon the material things about us; and it is reason still, only in a higher form, when we draw it out and give it a successional power, and behold through it that which lies beyond the region of the senses; and when we extend it to its utmost capacity, and the lenses are all right, we can look through it into heaven itself, and the magnificent background is the glory of God Almighty.

That state of mind in which a man is impressed with invisible things, is faith. It is the use of the mind and the soul power, in distinction from the body power. Men have such a narrow view of what faith is, that they look for it as one would look for a diamond; whereas they should look for it as treasure. Treasure may be precious stones, or gold, or raiment, or fragrant woods; treasure is a hundred things, diamond is but one; so faith is not a special thing, as many people make it. It does not apply to religion alone, but to all the departments of life. It is simply such a carriage of the soul as lifts it into the realm of the invisible, so that the man lives by his higher faculties, rather than by his lower. Even in the most practical matters, that man succeeds best who has the most of this element. The difference between a merchant prince and a petty trader is, that the trader can work only so far as he sees. He must be able to put his hand on cask, and box, and bale, while he whom we call the merchant prince, disdains to stop at what he can see and handle, but goes beyond and deals with the relations of things, and anticipates results, and taking into account time, and space, and quality, and quantity, and seasons, and races, and latitudes, he makes the whole earth minister to his need. This is commercial faith. In affairs of state, the man who looks only at forms of law, and at the daily routine of government, is but a politician; while he who comprehends those great, stately principles which walk, known or disguised, through all things, and who looks forth with clear vision to see the bearing of the present upon the future, is a statesman. This is political faith. There are many people who are so refined in their tastes, — and by refinement I mean the passage of a thing from a gross form to its evanishing point in the immaterial, — that they live in the ideal rather than in the actual. Such have an æsthetical faith. They have so cultivated their eye for colors that they can almost see the gleaming of the precious stones in the wall of heaven; and they have taught their ear so to appreciate harmonious sounds, that they can almost hear the celestial bells ringing sweet invitation to them; and they have so strengthened and purified their social natures that the fiery edges of heavenly affection almost touch theirs, as cloud lightning touches cloud lightning. How wretched will such be, when through death they really enter the realm of the invisible, to find that they have failed of the highest faith, the faith of the moral nature, which alone will admit them to the companionship of God!

May all of us have that faith in the Lord Jesus Christ which availeth, that faith which worketh by love, and so, though we have begun in the egg on earth, yet, through God's brooding, before we know it, we shall chip the shell; and though we have lain so long, coiled up and helpless, we shall begin to put forth plumes; and, disdaining the nest, and finding the ground chilly beneath our feet, with every gathering feather we shall pine for the air, and, pining, begin to try those notes which we are yet to learn; and, at length, in some bright and beaded morning, we shall spread our wings, and rising above the tangle and the thicket, soar through the blue, singing to the gate of heaven!

If we should gather all the flowers that grow upon the mountain sides and in the valleys, and heap them up before God, he would not be richer than he is now; but when we bring ourselves to him, and affection after affection opens and exhales in his presence, he is richer, and his joys are greater.

Many people seem to imagine that God keeps a gracious apothecary's shop above, with faith, and meekness, and humility put up in bottles ready for purchasers, and that, as they could go into a perfumer's here below, and ask for this or that extract, so they can go to God, and ask for this or that grace. They think if they go into their closet at night, and pray with faith for faith, if the expression be not an absurdity, that the next morning it will be delivered to them. Christian graces can never be obtained in this way. They must be the outgrowth of the life. The prayer for graces will be answered, but God will make us work out each one with fear and trembling. The spire that almost touches the stars, does not rise, isolated, from the ground; beneath it, and supporting it, is the massy substructure, the vast cathedral of stone. So faith cannot soar alone to heaven; it must be the steeple and spire of the whole life-building.

ALL true ambition and aspiration are without comparisons.

AS,—in some summer's morning which wakes with a ring of birds, when it is clear, leagues up into the blue, and every thing is as distinctly cut as if it stood in heaven and not on earth, when the distant mountains lie bold upon the horizon, and the air is full of the fragrance of flowers which the night cradled,—

the traveller goes forth with buoyant and elastic step upon his journey, and halts not till in the twilight shadows he reaches his goal, so may we, who are but pilgrims, go forth beneath the smile of God, upon our homeward journey. May heaven lie upon the horizon, luring us on; and when at last we sink to sleep, and dream that we behold again those whom we have lost, may we wake to find that it was not a dream, but that we are in heaven; and may the children for whom we have yearned, and the companions who anticipated us and gained heaven first, come to greet us. Then, sweeter than all, may we behold the face of the Lord Jesus, our Master, our Life, and cast ourselves before him, that he may raise us up with great grace, to stand upon our feet forevermore!

SOME men think that religion is a mere ecstatic experience, like a tune rarely played upon some faculty; living only while it is being performed, and then dying in silence. And, indeed, many men carry their religion as a church carries its bell — high up in a belfry, to ring out on sacred days, to strike for funerals, or to chime for weddings. All the rest of the time it hangs high above reach — voiceless, silent, dead. But religion is not the speciality of any one feeling, but the mood and harmony of the whole of them. It is the whole soul marching heavenward to the music of joy and love, with well-ranked faculties, every one of them beating time and keeping tune.

The religious life is thoughtful, but thought is not alone its nature. It is full of affection, but it has more than mere feeling; it abounds in grand moral impulses. Effervescent experiences are not its characteristic. It is the soul of a man made wondrously rich, moving to the touch of divine influence, in every way to which so facile and elaborate a creature as man can move. There is no end to its combinations. It shapes itself beyond all enumeration of shapes. It thinks in vast and fathomless streams. It wills with all attitudes of authority and decision. It feels with all moods and variations of social affection. It rises, by the wings of faith, into the invisible, and fashions for itself a life there, glowing with every imaginable ecstasy. And neither one of these is religion more than another. It is the whole soul's life that is religion. When the sun rose on Memnon, it was fabled to have uttered melodious noises; but what were the rude twangings of that huge, grotesque statue, compared with the soul's response when God rises upon it, and every part, like a vibrating chord, sounds forth, to his touch, its joy and worship?

Do men go to school because they know so much, or because they know so little? Do men go to a physician because they are sick, or do they wait till they are well and then go? Yet to hear people speak of uniting with the church one would suppose that they thought it their duty to stay out till they were perfect, and then to join it as ornaments. They who are weak, but who wish strength; they who are ignorant, but hunger for knowledge; they who are unable to go alone, and need sympathy and society to hold them up; they who are lame, and need crutches; in short, they who know the plague and infirmity of a selfish heart, a worldly nature, a sinful life, and who desire above all things to be lifted above them, have a preparation for the church. If you could walk without limping, why use a crutch at all? If you are already good enough, why go into a church? But if you are so lame that a staff is a help, so infirm that company and ordinances will aid you, then you have a right to the fellowship of the church. To unite with a church is not to profess that you are a saint, that you are good, and still less that you are better than others. It is but a public recognition of your weakness and your spiritual necessities. The church is not a gallery for the better exhibition of eminent Christians, but a chool for the education of imperfect ones, a nursery for the care of weak ones, a hospital for the better healing of those who need assiduous care.

How does one begin to learn Latin? Not charmed with the numbers of Virgil, but stumbling over the grammar; digging at roots of verbs. As it is with study, so it is with religion. No one should be disappointed if the early experiences of his Christian life involve many doubts and fears. A new life, like a new river, has to pick its way and find its channel. The waters will gather in pools, and seem to cease to flow. Rising over the brim, they will shoot through some rugged pass, and be swirled by a thousand jagged rocks; but by and by, when the channel is secured, and side streams begin to add their stores, the river will neither stop nor grow dry. There is no power on earth that can hold back the river from the ocean, or the Christian life from heaven.

God's promises were never meant to ferry our laziness. Like a boat, they are to be rowed by our oars; but many men, entering, forget the oar, and drift down more helpless in the boat than if they had staid on shore. There is not an experience in life by whose side God has not fixed a promise.

There is not a trouble so deep and swift-running, that we may not cross safely over, if we have courage to steer and strength to pull.

MANY of our troubles are God dragging us, and they would end if we would stand upon our feet, and go whither he would have us.

IN December the days grow shorter till the twenty-first, the shortest day, when, at a precise moment, the sun pauses and begins to return towards the north. And then, though the days are constantly growing longer, and the sun coming nearer, yet for weeks there is no apparent change. The snow lies heavy upon the earth. There are neither leaves, nor blossoms, nor singing birds; nothing to mark the summer time which is surely advancing. But at length the ground begins to relax in the sunny places, and the snows melt, and warm winds blow from the south, and buds swell, and flowers spring, and ere long there is the bloom and glory of June. So, there is a precise moment when the soul pauses in its departure from God, and begins to return towards him. The fruits of that return may not be at once visible; there may be long interior conflicts before the coldness and deadness of the heart is overcome; but at length the good will triumph, and instead of winter and desolation, all the Christian graces will spring up in the summer of divine love.

THE most you can do to a good man is to persecute him; and the worst that persecution can do is to kill him. And killing a good man is as bad as it would be to spite a ship by launching it. The soul is built for heaven, and the ship for the ocean, and blessed be the hour that gives both to the true element.

THERE are many persons who have heard so much of family government that they think there cannot be too much of it. They imprison their children in stiff rooms, where a fly is a band of music in the empty silence, and govern at morning, and govern at night, and the child goes all day long like a shuttle in the loom, back and forward, hit at both ends. Children subjected to such treatment are apt to grow up infidels, through mere disgusts.

THE Bible, without a spiritual life to interpret it, is like a trellis on which no vine grows — bare, angular, and in the way. The Bible, with a spiritual life, is like a trellis covered with a luxuriant vine — beautiful, odorous, and heavy with purple clusters shining through the leaves.

---

* I HAVE seen birds sitting on the boughs and watching while other birds were feeding below. They would hop from twig to twig, and look wistfully down upon them; then, gathering courage, they would spring from their perch and back again, and finding that it did not hurt them, they would at last join the outmost circle, and feed with the others. How many faces I have seen in these galleries, wearing a wistful look as they gazed down upon us while we were celebrating this ordinance of communion. May God give all such wings, that they may fly down and be among his people, and partake with them of heavenly food.

A MAN who should sit down to the communion table, having bitterness against a brother in his heart, would he not do wrong? "Yes," you answer at once. But it is communion every day. The body of Christ is wherever human bodies are,

* At communion.

and he who has any bitterness against his brother is always committing sacrilege.

A MISSIONARY sends home his children to be educated. They cannot be taught in the heathen country where he dwells, and so some sister receives the precious charge, and endeavors to supply to them the place of father and mother. They are very ignorant when they arrive, but they are trained and watched over with assiduous care. Teachers are provided for them; they are cultivated and developed on every side, and grow up to maturity, full of knowledge, and loveliness, and virtue. The time draws near when the parent shall come to claim them, and how anxious is their loving guardian lest he should be disappointed. Her constant thought is, "How shall I present these children acceptably to their father?"

As the ship that bears him approaches the land, the longing father can scarcely wait to clasp his dear ones in his arms. He makes haste to go on shore; he finds his sister's house, and when the first warm greetings are over, she leads him in with trembling joy, and says, "Here are your children!" and the son whom he left, a fair-haired boy, comes forward, dark-haired, deep-eyed, and taller than his father; and the daughter, who when he saw her last could do little but smile and cry, advances timidly, with blushing cheek, and all the grace of early womanhood. If they have been wayward and intractable, his love in that hour can overlook it all. If they have been docile and obedient, how gladly does he embrace them. But if, more than this, they have striven to improve every advantage, and to make themselves worthy of their father, and of the kind friend who has guided them, with what rapture does he fold them to his heart!

Christians are God's children whom he has sent to school upon earth, and Christ is their guide and teacher, who desires to present them to him "faultless," "without spot, or wrinkle, or any such thing." When, through death, the Father comes to take them home, how is Christ's heart grieved to present those who have been wayward and worldly; but they are children still, and the Father's love overlooks it, and they are "saved so as by fire." With subdued joy he presents those who have made no great attainments, but have yet been teachable and obedient, and they are welcomed to the heavenly inheritance. And then with radiant face he brings those shining bands who have been the true disciples, following gladly in the footsteps of the Master; pressing forward through toil and suffering to the prize, and the Father makes haste to greet them, and saying, "Come, ye blessed," folds them with rapture to his bosom!

The entering into heaven will reveal many things unknown on earth. Some whom the world thought saint-like will barely gain admittance there, and others who went all their lives in doubt and dread, will have angelic welcome, and an abundant entrance into the heavenly kingdom. "The first shall be last, and the last shall be first."

What do the flowers say to the night? They wave their bells, and exhale their choicest odors, as if they would bribe it to bestow upon them some new charm. In the tender twilight they look wistfully at each other, and say, "Do you see any thing on me?" and when the answer is, "I see nothing," they hang their heads and wait sorrowfully for the morning, fearing that they shall bring no beauty to it. Though there is no voice, nor sound, yet the night hears them, and silently through the still air the dews drop down from the sky, and settle on every stem, and bud, and blossom; and when day dawns, at the first rosy glance that the sun sends athwart the fields, ten million jewels glitter, and sparkle, and quiver on the notched edges of every leaf, and along each beaded blade and spire of grass, and spray, and the happy flowers, stirred by the wind, nod, and beckon, and smile to each other, more resplendent in their dewy gems than any dream of the night had imagined. So many Christians, who in the darkness of this life have longed and labored for graces, yet sad and fearing, will find themselves covered with glory when the eternal morning dawns, and the light of God's countenance strikes through their earth-gained jewels!

THERE are few men, even among the most worldly, who do not expect to be converted before they die; but it is a selfish, mean, sordid conversion they want—just to escape hell and to secure heaven. Such a man says, "I have had my pleasures, and the flames have gone out in the fireplaces of my heart. I have taken all the good on one side; now I must turn about if I would take all the good on the other." They desire just experience enough to make a key to turn the lock of the gate of the celestial city. They wish "a hope" just as men get a title to an estate. No matter whether they improve the property or not if they have the title safe. A "hope" is to them like a passport which one keeps quietly in his pocket till the time for the journey, and then produces it; or, like life preservers which hang useless around the vessel until the hour of danger comes, when the captain calls on every passenger to save himself, and then they are taken down and blown up, and each man with his hope under his arms strikes out for the land; and so, such men would keep their religious hope hanging idle until death comes, and then take it down and inflate it, that it may buoy them up, and float them over the dark river to the heavenly shore; or, as the inhabitants of Block Island keep their boats, hauled high upon the beach, and only use them now and then, when they would cross to the main land, so such men keep their hopes, high and dry upon the shore of life, only to be used when they have to cross the flood that divides this island of Time from the main land of Eternity.

As a man who is ignorant of the workmanship of a watch, tries to examine it, and after several bungling attempts succeeds in opening it, and then does not know where to find the mainspring or the hair-spring, or why the wheels play into each other, and at last shuts it again, so many men attempt self-examination. In the first place, they find it very hard to fix their thoughts. They cannot define their reason; they do not understand the play of their affections, or their moral powers, and so, after a weary hour they shut themselves up again, and hope that in some mysterious way God will bless to them the effort at self-examination. A man might as reasonably look into a well to see the sun rise, as to look thus into his heart with the expectation of good.

Other men examine themselves on this wise. They sit down and try to recall all their thoughts, and feelings, and actions during the day, and then they question themselves, "Do you enjoy reading the Bible?" Yes, they believe they do. "Do you like Sunday?" Yes, on the whole, what with the music and all the rest, they think they do like Sunday. "Are you fond of religious conversation?" Yes, if they can have their choice of people, they think they are fond of religious conversation. A vine would never be so stupid as to examine itself thus, but suppose it should, and should call out, "Roots, do you enjoy being down there in the soil?" "Yes, we enjoy being here in the soil." "Stem, do you like to be out there in summer?" "Yes, I like to be out here in summer." "Leaves, are you fond of waving in the sun and air?" "Yes, we are fond of the sun and air." and, satisfied, it says, "I am an excellent vine." But the gardener, standing near, exclaims, "The useless thing! I paid ten dollars for the cutting, and I have pruned and cultivated it, and for years looked for the black Hamburg grapes it was to bear, but it has yielded only leaves." He does not care that the roots love the soil, and the stem the summer. It makes no difference to him though every leaf spread itself broad as Sahara in its barrenness. It is fruit that he wants. Now, reading the Bible is like the roots in the soil, and liking Sunday is like the stem in summer, and being fond of religious conversation is like the leaves in the sun and air. If religion does not bring forth fruit in the life, all these things are as worthless in the sight of God, as is the barren vine in the thought of the gardener.

Around the *chef d'œuvres* in the galleries of Europe, artists are always congregated. You may see them standing before Raphael's Transfiguration, copying with the nicest care, every line and tint of that matchless work; glancing constantly from their canvas to the picture, that even in the minutest parts they may reproduce the original. But if at one side you saw an artist who only looked up occasionally from his work, and drew a line, but filled in here a tree or a waterfall, and there a deer or a cottage, just as his fancy suggested, what kind of a copyist would you call him? Now, true self-examination lies in ascertaining how nearly we are reproducing Christ. He is painted for us in no gallery, but his life glows, fourfold, in the Gospels, and our hearts are the canvas upon which we are to copy it. Let us not take occasional glimpses, and work, meanwhile, upon earthly designs; but let us look long and earnestly till our lives reflect the whole divine image.

COMING once down the Ohio River when the water was low, we saw just before us several small boats aground on a sandbar. We knew the channel was where they were not, and shaping our course accordingly, we went safely by. They saw our intention, and taking advantage of the light swell we created as we passed them, the nearest ones crowded on all steam and were lifted off the bar. Now, when in life's stream you are stranded on some bar of temptation, no matter what it is that makes a swell, if it is only an inch under your keel, put on all steam and swing off into the current. O, what joy to glide down the river between green and flowery banks, and to know that every hour is bringing you nearer home!

Our people, nomadic as the Arabs, impetuous as the Goths and Huns, pour themselves along our Western border, carrying with them all their wealth and all their institutions. They drive schools along with them as shepherds drive sheep, and troops of colleges go lowing over the Western plains, like Jacob's kine.

When I lived at the West, and preached sometimes every day and evening in the week, in order to rest myself, upon my return home, I often took up some botanical work and studied it, and in this way made myself acquainted with the history and cultivation of many plants which I had never seen. I even became a horticultural editor, and wrote familiarly of flowers which were known to me only through the botanist's description. When I came East, and went into a hothouse, I had to ask the names of the rarer plants, for I had never had their seeds, nor seen them growing in my garden. One flower particularly attracted my attention, and I said to the gardener,

"What is this?"

"A Marie Louise."

"But I do not know of what family it is."

He looked at me incredulously, for he had taken my paper, and supposed me learned in horticulture, as he answered,

"It is a cineraria, sir."

Now, there are many Christians who can talk learnedly of faith and humility, but who have never had them as seeds in their heart's garden, much less as perfect flowers, and who know so little of their real nature, that when they see them blooming in some rich Christian heart, they have to ask their names before they can recognize them.

THERE is no faculty of the human soul so persistent and universal as that of hatred. There are hatreds of race; hatreds of sect; social and personal hatreds. If thoughts of hatred were thunder and lightning, there would be a storm over the whole earth all the year round. Twenty people cannot be together, but some one suffers from their conversation. Let a man come into the company who from some cause is obnoxious to them, and no sooner does he depart than the ill-smelling flowers of hatred swell their buds, and give forth their malign influences through the room. Towards many people we live in a state of negative dislike, which requires only a spark to kindle into a positive flame of hatred. Now of all this Christ says, "Ye have heard that it hath been said, thou shalt love thy neighbor and hate thine enemy, but I say unto you, love your enemies." "Is there not an error in that translation?" you say, for when the Bible reads as people do not wish it to, they think there is some mistake in the Greek. No, there is no error in the translation. "But it only means that we should feel kindly towards them, and let them alone." Not at all. "Bless them that curse you, do good to them that hate you, and pray for them which despitefully use you and persecute you; that ye may be the children of your Father which is in heaven; for he maketh his sun to rise on the evil and on the good, and sendeth rain on the just and on the unjust." You must not only chain these thoughts of hatred and put them down into the dungeon, but you must call up a choir of sweet singers in their places. Every time your enemy fires a curse, you must fire a blessing, and so you are to bombard back and forth with this kind of artillery. The mother grace of all the graces is Christian good will.

THE pulpit should be like the key-board of an organ, and the church like the pipes. It is my business to press down the keys here, and it is yours to respond out there. Christian life ought to be so exhibitory that when you look at a Christian you will know what God's truth is. If one comes to me and asks the meaning of faith, and humility, and charity, I ought to be able to point to one man and say, "There is faith," and to another, "There is humility," and so on through all the church and all the graces. Christ's kingdom will not come until his disciples are such "living epistles, known and read of all men."

I BELIEVE there are many in this congregation who wake every morning to pray, and who never let the evening shadows go without perfuming them with their grateful thanks for the mercies of the day; who study their Bibles more than many professing Christians; and who believe that the life they now live is by faith in the Son of God, but who yet do not wish to have it known, and shrink from joining the church, and making a public acknowledgment of the debt they owe to Christ. They mean to *be* Christians, but not to avow themselves such. Thus they will leave the world to suppose that their manifest virtues are self-cultured, and that Christian lives may be led without Christ.

If I were a pupil of Titian, and he should design my picture, and sketch it for me, and look over my work every day and make suggestions, and then, when I had exhausted my skill, he should take the brush and give the finishing touches, bringing out a part here and there, and making the whole glow with beauty, and then I should hang it upon the wall and call it mine, what a meanness it would be! When life is the picture, and Christ is the designer and master, what greater meanness is it to allow all the excellences to be attributed to ourselves!

The engineer of an express train sees, just ahead, a switch wrongly turned, and knows that if he cannot stop the train it will go over the bank and be whelmed in instant destruction. The conductor jumps out, and the passengers after him, and run away across the fields; but the bold engineer resolves to share the fate of the engine. Speedily he reverses the action, and with all his strength rolls back the wheels. Just as the fatal point is reached, they cease to move, and, the train is saved! What meanness would it be, when, unharmed, they reach the town, for the conductor to say, "We were in great danger, but by my presence of mind I saved the train." Yet what greater meanness is it for us to take the credit to ourselves, when Christ saves us from the perils which lie in our way to eternity!

People sometimes say, "I am not a church member, but I am a better man than Mr. A, or Mr. B, who is." Perhaps you are; but it is Christ, through the minister and the church, who has made you so. God's influences come in upon you in mighty tides, and purify your life, and you have no right to claim for yourself the graces which belong to Christ.

A MAN might frame and let loose a star to roll in its orbit, and yet not have done so memorable a thing before God, as he who lets go a golden-orbed thought to roll through the generations of time.

Do you ask, "Why not do away with the church, if its members make so many mistakes?" Would you take away the lighthouse because careless mariners, through wrong observations, run their ships high and dry upon the shore? Would you put out the lamp in your house because moths and millers burn their wings in it? What would the children do?

IT would be a dreadful thing to me to lose my sight; to see no more the faces of those I love, nor the sweet blue of heaven, nor the myriad stars that gem the sky, nor the dissolving clouds that pass over it, nor the battling ships upon the sea, nor the mountains with their changing lines of light and shade, nor the loveliness of flowers, nor the burnished mail of insects. But I should do as other blind men have done before me; I should take God's rod and staff for my guide and comfort, and wait patiently for death to bring better light to nobler eyes. O ye who are living in the darkness of sin! turn before it is too late to the light of holiness, else death will bring to you, not recreation, but retribution. Earthly blindness can be borne, for it is but for a day; but who could bear to be blind through eternity?

As birds in the hour of transmigration feel the impulse of southern lands, and gladly spread their wings for the realm of light and bloom, so may we, in the death hour, feel the sweet solicitations of the life beyond, and joyfully soar from the chill and shadow of earth to fold our wings and sing in the summer of an eternal heaven!

It is a part of our physiological nature that in order to the healthful development of our moral faculties, they must be placed highest, else they can no more flourish than could a plant growing under the shade and drip of trees. But most men make no provision for these faculties. Like a lighthouse, built well from foundation upwards, but without any place for the lantern, so many men build carefully their lower natures, but never rear the highest story. As a musical instrument might have the base and tenor very well tuned and concordant, while, if you ran your fingers over the higher notes all would be clash and jargon, so men say, "I must compose and harmonize myself to natural laws for the sake of health," and thus they tune the base; and then they say, "I must have peace at home, and peace in my neighborhood," and so they regulate their social affections; and there are lofty flights of reason, and imagination, and art, and poetry, and music, and thus they tune the tenor; but when they come to the highest notes, which were meant to be sweet to the ear of God, there is neither regularity nor concordance. All is void, vast, and mysterious in their moral nature.

---

* It does my soul good to hear from you such cheerful testimony to the value of Christ's presence and blessing in affliction. At night, when a railroad train, having stopped at a station, is about to start

* At a church prayer meeting, where many had expressed their gratitude for God's sustaining grace in trial.

again, in order that the conductor may know that every thing is as it should be, the brakeman on the last car calls out through the darkness, "All right here!" and the next man takes up the word, "All right here!" and the next echoes, "All right here!" and so it passes along the line, and the train moves on. It does me good to sit here while you speak of the life you are guiding through the world's darkness, and pass the word from one to another, "All right here!" All is right every where when the heart is right.

THERE never was a ray of starlight in the Mammoth Cave of Kentucky; only the red glare of torches ever lights its walls. So there are many men whose minds are Mammoth Caves, all underground, and unlighted, save by the torches of selfishness and passion.

"THESE troublesome vines," exclaims the vintner, "why can they not grow upright like bushes?" And one man comes to him and says, "It is all because you have tied them to oak stakes. If you will get cedar stakes you will have no difficulty." The vintner goes to the forest for cedar stakes, but still the vines creep and cling. Another man says, "Cedar stakes are not good; you must have hickory;" and he gets hickory, but the vines clasp them also. Another man says, "It is not hickory, but chestnut stakes that you need;" and so he gets chestnut stakes, but it is all the same to the vines. At length there comes a man who says, "Your course is wrong from beginning to end. If you will throw away all your stakes, and stop your training, and leave the vines to nature, you will have none of these clambering, wild-roaming, embracing ways." So the vintner pulls up the stakes, and clears the piles of timber from the ground, and leaves the vines unpropped. And now do they grow upright, and cease to throw out tendrils and clasping rings? No. It is their nature to cling to something; and if you will not give them help to climb upward, they will not on that account cease to reach out, but will spread all over the ground, clasping cold stones, and embracing every worthless stick, and the very grass.

Now, our religious nature, like the vine, must have something to cling to; and one man says, "The Brahminical system is as good as the Christian;" and another says, "The old Greek mythology is better than either;" and another says, "Catholicism is preferable to the Protestant form of Christianity;" and then comes a man who declares that all systems are extraneous and hurtful, and that if we were left to grow up unprejudiced, with the light and laws of nature, such a thing as a religious system would never be known nor needed. "First," he says, "the nurse befools the child, and then the mother takes him, and then the priest and the church; and so he is educated to false views from the beginning." The truth of the matter is this: Religious systems do not create the religious nature in man. The religious nature itself, craving and longing for development, creates both the systems and the priests who minister in them. The heart, with its thousand tendrils, reaches forth to God, and in its reaching clasps whatever it may.

A student, annoyed by the notes of the canary bird in his window, says, "It is the robin in the opposite cage that makes the canary sing," and so he takes the robin away; but still the song goes on. It was not its companion that made it call, but something yearning out of its own little bosom; and because of this yearning, whether alone or with its mates, in summer or winter, in light or darkness, it still will sing. So the heart yearns and calls for God; not because of outward solicitation, but because of the longing, the want it feels within. No difference of teachers or systems can change this nature of the soul. The ocean is the same, whatever craft sail up and down upon it, whether they be pleasure boats, brigs, merchant ships, pirates, or men-of-war; so whatever religious navigators may be going up and down the sea of life, its depths, and shores, and distant haven remain the same. The stars never change for astrologers or astronomers. They roll calmly above storms and above opinions. So man's nature does not vary for circumstances, or conflicting views, but still wants God above, and fellow-man below.

Many of you are ashamed of these cravings. You know that you are never satisfied; that at every achievement your soul cries out for something more; but you will not acknowledge that these outreachings are homesicknesses for God. I know you will not bear to be told this directly, and so, being crafty, I catch you with guile; and sometimes by memories of childhood, and sometimes by perils of manhood, sometimes by love, and sometimes by fear, I seek to gain your attention, and to show you that your great want is God. There are bells in your soul which God has hung, and which were meant to sound forth his praise but you say, "No; there shall be no chime;" and you cut off the ropes, so that they cannot be rung. If I can I will steal up to the belfry, and with good blows will make them speak; and if that is not permitted, I will yet throw up words from without, as boys cast stones, to strike the mute bells and arouse their echoes.

Many will say, "I can find God without the help of Bible, or church, or minister." Very well. Do so if you can. The Ferry Company would feel no jealousy of a man who should prefer to swim to New York. Let him do so, if he is able, and we will talk about it on the other shore; but probably trying to swim would be the thing that would bring him quickest to the boat. So God would have no jealousy of a man's going to heaven without the aid of Bible, or church, or minister; but let him try to do so, and it will be the surest way to bring him back to them for assistance.

However various our wants may seem, what we all need is God. He has given us the earth for our body, but he himself is the soil in which our souls must root; the eternal help, the source of succor and all supply, the bread of life, and the water of life. Feeding upon him, we shall hunger no more, neither thirst any more, but be satisfied.

A SHIP that has been driven by wave and tempest far up on the beach, where no tide can ever come to lift her off, but that lies there, high and dry, seams gaping, sails rotting, spars falling, hated of earth and driven out from the water, is not half so pitiable an object as a great man who by policy, policy, policy, has been carried out of the deep channels of honor and lies all awreck upon the shore of good men's opinions.

If I had been made a firefly, it would not become me to say, "If God had only made me a star, to shine always, then I would shine." It is my duty, if I am a firefly, to fly and sparkle, and fly and sparkle; not to shut my wings down over my phosphorescent self, because God did not make me a sun or a star.

The tides come twice a day in New York harbor, but they only come once in seven days in God's harbor of the sanctuary. They rise on Sunday, but ebb Monday, and are down and out all the rest of the week. Men write over their store door, "Business is business," and over the church door, "Religion is religion," and they say to religion, "Never come in here," and to business, "Never go in there." "Let us have no secular things in the pulpit," they say; "we get enough of them through the week in New York. There all is stringent and biting selfishness, and knives, and probes, and lancets, and hurry, and work, and worry. Here we want repose, and sedatives, and healing balm. All is prose over there; here let us have poetry. We want to sing hymns and to hear about heaven and Calvary; in short, we want the pure gospel, without any worldly intermixture." And so they desire to spend a pious, quiet Sabbath, full of pleasant imaginings and peaceful reflections; but when the day is gone, all is laid aside. They will take by the throat the first debtor whom they meet, and exclaim, "Pay me what thou owest! It is Monday." And when the minister ventures to hint to them something about their duty to their fellow-men, they say, "O you stick to your preaching. You do not know how to collect your own debts, and cannot tell what a man may have to do in his intercourse with the world." God's law is not allowed to go into the week. If the merchant spies it in his store, he throws it over the counter. If the clerk sees it in the bank, he kicks it out at the door. If it is found in the street, the multitude pursue it, pelting it with stones, as if it were a wolf escaped from a menagerie, and shouting, "Back with you! You have got out of Sunday!" There is no religion in all this. It is mere sentimentalism. Religion belongs to every day; to the place of business as much as to the church.

High in an ancient belfry there is a clock, and once a week the old sexton winds it up; but it has neither dial plate nor hands. The pendulum swings, and there it goes, ticking, ticking, day in and day out, unnoticed and useless. What the old clock is, in its dark chamber, keeping time to itself, but never showing it, that is the mere sentimentality of religion, high above life, in the region of airy thought; perched up in the top of Sunday, but without dial or pointer to let the week know what o'clock it is, of Time, or of Eternity!

Many persons hang themselves on some crotchet or text in the closet, as a pot is hung over a slow fire, simmering and waiting to boil. They heap up their experiences for fuel, and wait for the time to come when they shall be so heated that they shall boil over in prayer. This may sometimes be a profitable religious exercise, but those who practise it should not deem it the only one, and make it tyrannize over all the rest.

EVERY man in a Christian church ought to feel that he uses the power of the whole, yet never so as to take away from him the need of individual exertion. If we have experience, any brother has a right to come to us and say, "Put your experience, as a bridge, over that stream which I must cross. I want timber there to walk on."

MEN secrete their religious life through shame, or fear of criticism, or morbid sensibility; but no man can be a Christian without being luminous. A man may carry his faith so guardedly that no one shall suspect that he is a Christian; but the worst of this is, that God never suspects it either, and forgets to write down his name in the Book of Life.

A MAN'S house should be on the hill-top of cheerfulness and serenity, so high that no shadows rest upon it, and where the morning comes so early, and the evening tarries so late, that the day has twice as many golden hours as those of other men. He is to be pitied whose house is in some valley of grief between the hills, with the longest night and the shortest day. Home should be the centre of joy, equatorial and tropical.

The whole force of life and experience goes to prove that right or wrong doing, whether in relation to the physical or the spiritual nature, is sure, in the end, to meet its appropriate reward or punishment. Penalties are often so long delayed, that men think they shall escape them; but some time they are certain to follow. When the whirlwind sweeps through the forest, at its first breath, or almost as if the fearful stillness that precedes had crushed it, the giant tree with all its boughs falls, crashing, to the ground. But it had been preparing to fall for twenty years. Twenty years before it had received a gash. Twenty years before the water commenced to settle in at some crotch, and from thence decay began to reach in with its silent fingers towards the heart of the tree. Every year the work of death progressed, till at length it stood, all rottenness, only clasped about by the bark with a semblance of life, and the first gale felled it to the ground. Now, there are men who for twenty years have shamed the day and wearied the night with their debaucheries, but who yet seem strong and vigorous, and exclaim, "You need not talk of penalties. Look at me! I have revelled in pleasure for twenty years, and I am as hale and hearty to-day as ever." But in reality they are full of weakness and decay. They have been preparing to fall for twenty years, and the first disease strikes them down in a moment.

Ascending from the physical nature of man to the mind and character, we find the same laws prevail. People sometimes say, "Dishonesty is as good as honesty, for aught I see. There are such and such men who have pursued for years the most corrupt courses in their business, and yet they prosper, and are getting rich every day." Wait till you see their end. Every year how many such men are overtaken with sudden destruction, and swept forever out of sight and remembrance! Many a man has gone on in sin, practising secret frauds and villanies, yet trusted and honored, till at length, in some unsuspected hour, he is detected, and, denounced by the world, he falls from his high estate as if a cannon ball had struck him, — for there is no cannon that can strike more fatally than outraged public sentiment, — and flies over the mountains, or across the sea, to escape the odium of his life. He believed that his evil course was building him up in fame and fortune; but financiering is the devil's forge, and his every act was a blow upon the anvil shaping the dagger that should one day strike home to his heart and make him a suicide. The pea contains the vine, and the flower, and the pod, in embryo, and I am sure, when I plant it, that it will produce them and nothing else. Now, every action of our lives is embryonic, and according as it is right or wrong, it will surely bring forth the sweet flowers of joy, or the poison fruits of sorrow. Such is the constitution of this world, and the Bible assures us that the next world only carries it forward. Here and hereafter, "whatsoever a man soweth, that shall he also reap."

The young sometimes say, "By and by we mean to separate the evil from the good, and to become religious; but first we wish a little liberty for enjoyment." At the mouth of the Mississippi, where it pours its immense flood into the Gulf of Mexico, how impossible would it be to stay the flow of its waters, and to separate from each other the drops of the various streams that have poured into it on either side — of the Red River, the Arkansas, the Ohio, and the Missouri; or to sift grain by grain from the detritus, the particles of sand that have wasted from the Ozark, or the Alleghany, or the far Rocky Mountains; yet how much more impossible would it be, when character is the river, and habits, formed one after another, are the side streams, to throw a little dam of conversion across, and separate the bad from the good! Let the stream run pure from its source. What if the farmer should mix cockles and other vile weeds with the wheat, and say, "When the grain is ripe, I will go in with sickle, and cradle, and winnowing machine, and separate them." Would it not be easier to sow clean wheat than to cleanse dirty wheat? You who are young are now at the sowing end of the harvest field. Scatter only pure seed, that when you reach the reaping end you may find no tares, but only the golden grain.

WHAT a thrifty, robust plant is the potato when out in the field it grows beneath the sun! Its leaf so coarse and green, its stem so stout and succulent, it is a pleasure to look upon a thing which seems so to take hold of all the elements of life. But when it has sprouted in the cellar, which has but one north window, half closed, it is a poor, cadaverous, etiolated, melancholy vine, growing up to that little flicker of light; sickly, blanched, and brittle.

Like the cellar-growing vine is the Christian who lives in the darkness and bondage of fear. But let him go forth, with the liberty of God, into the light of love, and he will be like the plant in the field, healthy, robust, and joyful.

As the pilot boats cruise far out, watching for every whitening sail, and hover through day and night, all about the harbor, vigilant to board every ship, that they may bring safely through the Narrows all the wanderers of the ocean, so should we watch off the gate of Salvation, for all the souls, tempest tossed, beating in from the sea of Sin, and guide them through the perilous straits, that at last, in still waters, they may cast the anchor of their hope.

A FATHER, with his little son, is journeying overland to California, and when at night he pitches his tent in some pleasant valley, the child is charmed with the spot, and begs his father to rear a house and remain there; and he begins to make a little fence about the tent, and digs up the wild flowers and plants them within the enclosure. But the father says, "No, my son. Our home is far distant. Let these things go, for to-morrow we must depart." Now, God is taking us, his children, as pilgrims and strangers, homeward; but we desire to build here, and must be often overthrown before we can learn to seek "the city that hath foundations, whose Builder and Maker is God."

THE sweetest music is not the peal of marriage bells, nor tender descants in moonlight woods, nor trumpet notes of victory — it is the soul's welcome to heaven. God grant that when we die there may not come booming to our ear the dreadful sound, "Depart!" but may we hear, stealing upon the air, the mellow chime of all the celestial bells, saying, "Come, come, come, ye blessed, enter ye into the joy of your Lord!"

THERE is no tyranny more intolerable than a conscience unrestrained by love. Like an ill-loaded gun, it recoils at the breech and kills at the muzzle. A conscience unsubdued by love torments the owner, and bruises those upon whom he lets it loose.

TAKE a sharp-cut young saint, just crystallized, as many-pointed and as clear as a diamond, and how good he is! how decided for the right, and how abhorrent of wrong! He abhors evil rather than loves good. He has not yet attained to the meekness and gentleness of Christ. But years will teach him that love is more just than justice; that compassion will cure more sins than condemnation; and that summer will do more, with silent warmth, to redeem the earth from barrenness, than winter can, with all the majesty of storms and the irresistible power of her icy hand.

WHEN we receive a grace, it is not because God, out of his infinite stores, takes a grace and hands it down to us, but because it is produced in our life. As pictures are slid into a magic lantern, and then reflected upon a wall, so many people think God slides graces into the heart, and that the man's life only reflects them. But graces are not interjected pictures. Their forms and colors are the substance of the heart. The engineer does not bring the journey to the locomotive; the locomotive produces it. When a watch is rightly constructed, God does not put time into it hour by hour; the regular working of the machinery, so far as the watch is concerned, makes and marks the time. Now, religion, the sum of the graces, is making the right journey heavenward — keeping time to God.

MORALITY must always precede and accompany religion, and yet religion is much more than morality. You buy a camellia, and determine, in spite of florists, to make it blossom in your parlor. You watch and tend it, and at length the buds appear. Day by day you see them swell, and fondly hope they will come to perfect flower; but just as they should open, one after another they drop off; and you look at it, despairingly exclaiming, "All is over for this year!" But I say, "What! the plant is thrifty. Are not Japonica roots, and branches, and leaves good?" "Yes," you answer; "but I do not care for them. I bought it for the blossom." Now, when we bring God the roots, and branches, and leaves of morality, he is not satisfied. He wants the blossoming of the heart; and that is religion.

To a Christian who has lived all his life long in bondage unto fear, not daring to believe himself a child of God, how sweet will be the waking in heaven! With great dread and trembling he will approach the death hour, and go down through chilling mists and vapors to the unknown sea. And when upon the other shore sweet strains come to his ear, he will not understand them; but fair form after fair form will appear to greet him, and at length, from the impearled atmosphere, God's whole band of gathering and reaping angels, more in number than the autumn leaves out-streaming from the forest when there are bursts of wind, will come forth, filling all the air with music, and minister unto him an abundant entrance into the heavenly kingdom! It were almost enough to make one's heaven, to stand and see the first wild stirring of joy in the face, and hear the first rapturous cry as they cross the threshold, of thousands of timid Christians who lived weeping and died sighing, but who will wake to find every tear an orb of joy, and every sigh an inspiration of God. O, the wondrous joy of heaven to those who did not expect it!

A CHILD lies in his little bed in some high chamber of an old castle, and hears the tempest growling in the chimney, and the prowling thief-winds at the window, and the scream of the spirits of the air. The storm rocks the walls and beats upon the roof, and he shudders, and covers his head, and expects at every burst of thunder that the castle will go crashing to the ground. But down in the room below, his father sits unmoved, reading by the fire, only now and then, when the tempest swells, he raises his spectacles for a moment, and exclaims, "God help the poor wretches on the sea to-night!" or, "I hope no belated traveller is out in such a storm as this," and then turns to his book again. In the morning the child hardly dares to look forth lest the heavens and the earth have passed away; but the father only walks into his garden, to see if some old tree has been blown down, or some unpropped vine fallen from the trellis.

In times of peril and disaster, the Christian,

through his faith and hope in God, is like the father by the fire, while he who has no such trust is tormented with fear and apprehension, like the child in the chamber. Let him who will, swelter in his philosophic anguish; I will rest in the serenity of Christian hope.

You pray for the graces of faith, and hope, and love; but prayer alone will not bring them. They must be wrought in you through labor, and patience, and suffering.

A garden has heard that the royal garden has a fountain, and sends up a petition to the head gardener that it may have a fountain too. He favors the request, and comes with workmen and the necessary implements to make it. The flower beds are torn up, the turf is cut and removed, the earth is thrown out in piles, and the astonished garden exclaims, "What is this? you are killing all my violets and roses." And now the boring commences, down through the quicksand and the surface soil, till a bed of rock is gained. Then, when the severer drilling begins, the terrified garden cries out, "My foundations will be destroyed! I thought I was to have a fountain." A small stream of water appears, but the gardener knows it would not always flow, and so he penetrates the earth yet farther, till at last, hundreds of feet below the surface, he reaches unfailing springs. Now the pipes are brought, and when they are adjusted, the earth is thrown back, the stones are removed, the turf is replaced, the ground is swept, and the flowers returned to their beds; and day in and day out the fountain plays, falling into its marble basin with ceaseless shower. The plants revive in its cooling spray, the birds come to sing to its music, and the whole garden rejoices in its beauty.

Now, who is willing that God should bore in his heart for the graces of faith, and hope, and love? You pray for them, but when God begins to work, you cry out, "O Lord! save my flower beds. You are killing all my violets and roses." Yet only through this working are the wells of salvation dug in our hearts, and the living waters made to flow.

"Now abideth Faith, Hope, Love, these three; but the greatest of these is Love," for love is the seraph, and faith and hope are but the wings by which it flies.

www.ingramcontent.com/pod-product-compliance
Lightning Source LLC
LaVergne TN
LVHW022039110826
845151LV00007B/864

* 9 7 8 1 4 2 5 5 3 1 2 0 1 *